Trust Me

by Blake O'Connor

Trust Me
by Blake O'Connor
Copyright © 2015. All Rights Reserved

ISBN 13: 978-0-9889409-5-6

Edited by Felicia A. Sullivan
Co-edited by Courtney Gremmel
Interior design by MPP Freelance

Praise for Blake O'Connor

"What an amazing book. Rarely have I been moved in such a way. I could read this book 10 times and still love it. If you love dogs, believe in overcoming grief and finding true love, this book is for you!"

"It was well written and will definitely recommend it to many friends! Couldn't put it down! I'm on to the next book by Blake O'Connor!"

"Beautifully written, each sentence was so simple, yet elegantly woven."
    – Pamela Sparkman, author of the *Stolen Breaths* series

Other award winning titles by Blake O'Connor

Unspoken Bond
Miracle on Wolf Hollow Lane

Dedicated to my husband, Alan, and my daughters
Michelle and Courtney. You are my world.

And to all the pets that have graced my life:
Monte, Michael, Skippy, Beagle, Big Boy, Daisy,
Buttons, Sandy, Glenda, Tony, Mitsi, Wendy, and Bat

Chapter 1

He was alone again, and with each passing day the male dog struggled to live.

Abandoned at a rest stop, he was left to fend for himself. He had made a shelter in a hollowed log by scratching and scruffing the softened bark until it molded to his shape. Days turned into weeks, and weeks into months, and this would be his last day in the hollowed log he called home.

He was a two year old dog, had an intimidating size, and dark colored coat. His eyes blazed and his black Labrador heritage from his father's side commanded attention. His mother had descended from hound dogs, passing down intelligence and cunning to her male offspring.

He had survived by drinking water from a creek and scavenging food from trashcans at the rest stop where he had been dumped. It was a pathetic way to survive, yet the dog persevered.

One night, two months prior, as the male dog lay hidden in the bushes, he observed an unsteady man walking toward him. In his hand he held a sack. The man hugged the shadows, staying away from the bright lights illuminating the darkest spots of the rest stop.

Something inside the sack wiggled and whimpered,

garnering the attention of the male dog.

The man stopped, pulled a shiny flask from his back pocket, and took a swig. Afterward, he hocked spit onto the cement then wiped his mouth with the back of his hand. When a light breeze came through, the dog got a whiff of cheap booze.

The man came to the back boundary of the rest stop and reached into the bag. He cursed when his hand came into contact with wetness, his face scrunching into an expression of utter disgust.

With a rough hand he jerked a small, fluffy white female dog out of the bag, holding her tight by the scruff of her neck. She quivered at the sight of the man, struggling against his hands.

Pee dribbled down the sides of her legs, and her eyes went wide with fear as she looked at the man and at the unfamiliar surroundings.

"I should have gotten rid of you long ago, *Butterball*."

The man laughed, and with a flippant toss, he hurled the petrified dog high into the air, throwing her over the barbed wire fence as if she was a sack of garbage. She hit a tree limb, legs flailing in the air before she fell onto a pile of hard sticks and other debris. She yelped and struggled to get up.

The male dog was helpless to intervene or protest, knowing if he showed himself, kicks or yells would follow.

He crawled out from his hiding place and went to where the cruel man had been, sniffing the air, snarling at him as he ran away. The man had a peculiar gait, different from other men the dog was used to seeing. He stepped high like the horses did in the adjacent pastures. He held his head and nose in the air, acting superior, as if the world was his kingdom, there only for his taking.

The dog bared his teeth and growled low, the raised

ruff on his back announcing his mistrust. The scent trail of sweat and booze was unmistakable, and unadulterated meanness lingered in the air.

It was a scent branded into the dog's memory.

It was a scent he would never forget.

He trotted over to the female dog and nosed her. Afraid of the larger dog, she rolled over and showed her underbelly, acquiescing to his dominance. She peed again. He sniffed her, taking in her smell. As a house dog, she had lived a life of comfort, curled on a sofa, and at one time she had been loved unconditionally by her mistress.

Except for the bruising caused by landing on the pile of sticks, she was otherwise healthy and had recently eaten.

The male dog sensed the little dog had lived a while without her mistress, and instead had cowered in the presence of the cruel man, afraid of his hand and voice.

Gently, the male dog nosed her, encouraging her to leave the debris pile. He herded her toward the log he called home, following close behind her. She was hesitant to enter the darkened log, and looked back at the male dog for confirmation.

He nudged her inside where he curled next to her, offering her the warmth of his body. Her fur was white and curly, her nose black against her sweet face. She was the kind of dog suited for a lap by a warm fire, not one who could live long outside in the brutal elements.

He licked her bruised leg and nibbled at the matted fur behind her ears. Using his teeth, he pulled a stick out of her curly fur, licking until he was satisfied, and when he was finished he put his head close to her.

Gradually that night she came to trust him, and before dawn broke she fell into a deep sleep.

They stayed together for weeks, keeping each other company, foraging for food and water. She relied on his strength to protect her. A pair, they had bonded, each giving the other a reason to live.

One day when the sun was high in the sky, the female dog left the safety of the log to search for food on her own. The male dog had stayed behind, being too wary of human interaction to venture out during daytime when the rest stop filled with noisy travelers.

Hidden in the log, he apprehensively watched the activity at the wayward place, waiting for his companion to return. Worried she had been gone for so long, he barked for her to return, but in the confusion of cars and caterwauling kids, she had not heard him.

The little female dog, famished from hunger, her eyesight blurry, had wobbled to the doors leading to the restrooms. Panting, she sat down, and too weak to stay upright, she collapsed on the hard concrete floor.

A girl screamed and called for her father. He rushed to her side to find the small white dog on its side. Her eyes were glazed, her breathing difficult. Conversation was hushed and the father put his arms around his young daughter trying to comfort her. She cried, wailing for her father to help the dog. Regardless of what he said, the little girl was inconsolable.

After much wailing and crying, the father whispered something in his daughter's ear. The tears magically disappeared. The father left and when he returned he carried a box lined with towels he had in one of the moving boxes in his car. He bent down and scooped up the unconscious little dog and placed her in the box. He instructed his daughter to stay close and follow him to their car. The girl skipped behind, smiling, keeping a keen eye on the fluffy white dog.

The male dog watched from a distance, pacing back and forth along the hollow log, unsure what to do. When the man took the little dog, the male dog bolted to the barbed wire fence. The man and the girl got in a car and left, unaware of the drama that had unfolded.

The male dog followed the car as it turned on the highway, and he raced the length of the fence until the car gained speed and disappeared over a hill.

Out of breath and panting, the dog stood at the edge of the woods, alone again.

For hours he waited by the side of the road, watching, hoping his companion would return. When nightfall came, he slunk back to his hollowed log, defeated.

Days turned into weeks, and then a month. The female dog never returned. The male dog waited and watched, just like he had done waiting for his owner to return, to reclaim him, to help him.

Weariness of living alone had taken a toll on the male dog, and he rarely ventured from his hollowed log to search for food. Death would be welcome, releasing him from the nagging pain in his stomach and the loneliness in his soul.

The male dog was of mixed breed and had at one time possessed a beautiful stature and shiny coat. He now shivered in a dull, matted carpet of fur in the hollow log. He had learned a long time ago to be wary of any approaching human at the rest stop. Strangers never had good intentions.

Thirst and hunger once again drove him to approach the travelling humans. He had become emaciated from the lack of food, losing half his weight. His eyes became dull, his hip and rib bones protruded.

Unaware of his intimidating size and rabid appearance, his approach was met with hurled objects and screams from frightened mothers pushing their children away. Angry fathers charged at him and shouted obscenities. After enduring these scary encounters, he gave up on trying to re-enter the human world.

A faint glimmer of fortitude lingered, and the dog

still possessed a will to live.

This night as he lay hidden in the hollowed log, movement alerted him, and he watched a man walk toward him.

Chapter 2

At six feet tall, Brendon McMahon was one of those men who commanded respect whenever he walked into a room. He was the type of man women wanted, and men wanted to emulate.

The thirty year old was driving home to the ranch he had inherited from his parents. He had given away whatever meager furnishings he had accumulated, and had packed his truck with all his remaining worldly belongings, which now fit into a couple of duffle bags.

He felt unencumbered with meaningless possessions and things that didn't matter. If only he could rid his mind of his troubles, life would be better.

What mattered now was the Greyhound bus that had unloaded a cargo full of retirees minutes before Brendon decided he needed to stop at the rest stop.

Driving west on Interstate 10 from Houston, Brendon took a bite out of his ham and cheese sandwich. Thirsty from the day's work of cleaning his apartment so he could get his deposit back, he had already polished off two bottles of water on the drive. Looking around for another drink, he spied the thermos he had packed. Taking a swallow, he washed the bite of sandwich down with the last bit of coffee.

Brendon soon reached overload on the amount of liquid he had consumed, innately aware of the uncomfortable pressure of nature calling. He decided it was time for a pit stop.

Pulling his truck into a space at the end of the rest stop parking lot, Brendon groaned at his timing when he spotted the whale of a bus parked curbside. He surveyed the long line of graying men dressed in Hawaiian shirts and khaki pants standing outside the restroom.

"Great," he muttered.

He sat there a few minutes, wiggling awkwardly in his seat, mulling over how long he could wait.

Not long, he decided.

Fortunately it was getting dark, and the sun had slid behind the trees, casting long shadows over the land. Low clouds ribboned across the horizon, softening the sky with colors of faded quilts and late summer roses.

Darkness would cover him.

Swinging open the driver's door of his truck, he nonchalantly strolled around the side of the concrete building which housed the restrooms. He dipped his chin at the lady walking her dog, then hightailed it to the corner of the one acre plot carved out of the surrounding woodland.

He discreetly checked his surroundings, making sure he wasn't being noticed. Everyone was busy.

Pinching down the top rung of the barbed wire fence, Brendon leaned forward and swung his right leg over, then his left. He checked if anyone was looking.

So far, so good.

He ducked behind a stand of trees, wove his way through some bushes and deadfalls, and stepped into the darkness of the leaf-covered ground. He unzipped his pants.

Relief, at last.

The man hopped the fence. Leaves rustled and branches scraped against his clothes.

The male dog lowered his head, resting his chin on his front paws. Instinct guided the dog to remain still and quiet in the safety of his dark, dank abode.

The man walked right by the hollow log and stopped inches away, facing a tree. He mumbled something as he unzipped his pants.

Like so many male humans had done before this man, he urinated.

The dog lifted his nose at the odor filling the air providing valuable information needed about this man.

Sniff, sniff.

The man was in the prime of his life, healthy, with strong bones and constitution. He had eaten a ham sandwich and had recently consumed coffee, a scent that brought back comforting memories to the dog of a warm kitchen filled with the aromas of sizzling bacon and laughing children.

For a moment the dog was content until his belly ached from lack of food. The memories evaporated.

Wary, the dog crouched lower and continued to study the man.

After the man finished his business, he let out a satisfied sigh, zipped up his pants, and took a step backward without looking.

The man's boot caught on a branch hidden by leaves and he stumbled, arms windmilling about. All 200 pounds of man fell on the hollowed log that was the dog's home.

The dog winced at the commotion and at the thud the man's head made when it hit hard, knobby bark.

The man made a grunting sound as he rolled over on his back. He closed his eyes and became still in the low light.

Frightened, the dog's eyes became wide, his senses heightened, and he used them to assess the situation.

It was quiet, sans the low murmurings from the rest

stop. Weary parents escorted sleepy children to the restrooms; dogs barked and whined, communicating in the way they do; engines revved; and the dog continued looking at the man, lying inches away.

The sun slid further behind the horizon. Long shadows danced in the woods and on the buildings of the rest stop.

Sniff, sniff.

The man interested the dog.

The dog checked his surroundings for movement or signs of any close human activity. He sensed all human activity was at the rest stop, so with great trepidation, the dog left the safety of the log.

On the damp, leaf-covered ground the dog took a silent step toward the man. He swung his nose in the air, tasting the man's essence, listening to the rhythmic beating of his heart. He smelled of honest sweat and spices from food he had eaten that day. Smelled of the city and cars.

The dog took another unsure step, and his eyes went to the man's hands. They were the hands of a man who was honest and kind; a man who wouldn't raise his hand in anger or frustration.

He licked the man's fingertips, tentatively at first and then he licked all along the man's fingers, tasting the activities of the day.

Myriad cleaning smells lingered on his hands, those of soap and stronger detergents. Lemon-scented furniture polish and grease-cutting agents tickled the dog's nose.

The dog put his nose closer to the man, and he sniffed along his pants, up his side then to his head.

A trickle of blood ran down the side of the man's face. The dog canted his head, taking in the familiar smell. As the dog observed the wounded man, an overwhelming need to lick the man came over the dog. The human needed help, so the dog acted accordingly and did what came natural to him.

Lick, lick.

He licked to clean the man and to comfort him, like he had done to the little white fluffy dog who had been his companion. The warm tongue massaged the man's face, and removed the crimson stain. In those few moments of licking the man, the dog came to know more about the man, tasting the very essence of his body.

While the man's body was obviously strong, there was sadness in his soul that seeped out in his blood. Some type of emotional trauma the man had been through, and the dog tasted the internal struggle the man was fighting. The dog sensed the struggle had been lengthy and had taken a heavy toll on the man, yet the man fought it, and had become stronger despite the turmoil.

Like the dog, the man was a fighter. Not of brawn, which could be used when needed, but of an inner strength. The man had purpose and was on a mission, though of what, the dog could not understand.

He was a man the dog wanted to trust, but the dog wasn't sure how to trust after being betrayed in the most inhumane way. Being close to the man revived a tiny amount of faith the dog still had left in the human race. The dog desperately needed a companion, someone to guide him, to believe in him. He needed to be part of a pack again.

Movement!

The dog jumped back.

The man's fingers twitched, the index finger first, followed by a curling hand. Simultaneously, the man's eyes opened to a fuzzy and dark world.

He moaned and uttered unintelligible words.

He raised a hand to his head and carefully inspected his forehead, running his fingers through his hair, touching his scalp. He groaned when he felt a large lump and matted down hair.

Unafraid, the dog sat on his haunches, studying the man's purposeful movements.

The man bent a knee of one leg then the other, reached to the ground with one hand, and rolled up to a sitting position. For a moment he did nothing while the dog continued to sit to the side, observing the man.

The man shook his head but the movement only made his head throb worse, so he lay back down on the ground.

Brendon couldn't quite understand what had happened. The last thing he remembered after peeing was the thought he hadn't been noticed. Maybe he had gotten robbed and hit over the head, which would explain the large lump. He checked his back pants' pocket, which still had his wallet, and neither were his keys missing, so robbery was definitely ruled out.

Brendon ran his hands over his chest and midsection, checking if he had been shot. Nope, no bullet wounds, and he certainly knew about those and what they felt like.

A twinge of a memory tingled his chest where one of the bullets had hit him. He still had the scars on his chest reminding him of the close call with death on that fateful day two years prior when he had to discharge his service pistol during the commission of an armed robbery. A man had died and Brendon had been consumed with guilt ever since, quitting the police force, shunning friends and colleagues. It was his own self-imprisonment and was one of the driving forces behind him leaving Houston.

He breathed in the night air, thinking he had no clue how long he had been unconscious. As he lay on his back, his head throbbing, he stared at the canopy of trees above him and became aware of a log a few feet away.

The rest stop, yards away, had become quiet at this late night hour, and for some reason he felt like someone or something was staring at him, and hard.

It unnerved him.

Brendon remained still, letting his eyes adjust to the dark, and when he turned his head he spotted a form near him. He took a second look.

It was a dog, sitting on its haunches, staring straight at him.

The dog didn't make a sound, though even in the low light, Brendon could discern the dog was thin. He felt immediate empathy for the dog, probably a pet that had been dumped at the rest stop. By the looks of him he had probably been on his own for a while, scared and wary of humans, so Brendon didn't make any quick movements.

Brendon sat up and made clicking noises, hoping to entice the dog closer so he could get a better look at him, or at least he thought it was a *him*.

"Come here, boy," Brendon said. "Come here. It's okay. I'm not going to hurt you."

The dog timidly looked around as if seeking permission to move.

"Come on," Brendon urged. "You can do it. Come on."

When the dog didn't move, Brendon scooted a few inches toward the dog. He talked in low, soothing tones without making eye contact.

A few minutes had gone by of Brendon talking, of the dog sitting on his haunches, so when Brendon got within arm's length, he held out his arm, fingers stretched.

The dog craned his neck and sniffed.

"Do you mind if I get a little closer?" Brendon asked. He wasn't expecting an answer, only trying to get the dog used to his voice.

A few more inches of scooting and Brendon was close

enough to get a good look.

"Oh," he breathed out. "How can anyone do this to a dog?" Brendon shook his head in disgust. The dog was pitifully thin and he had a sore on his leg. "Get in a fight lately? By the looks of it, I would say yes. Can I look at your leg?"

Brendon reached, gently touching the dog's front leg. It was scabby and the dog pulled his leg back.

"I'm not going to hurt you. You can trust me. Promise."

Brendon examined the leg, kneading it, feeling for any broken bones. He touched the dog's hind quarters, still muscled, yet in dire need of nutrition.

"You must have been a beauty at one time, weren't you? I bet you're hungry too. Stay here and I'll be right back. I'll get you some water and something to eat."

The dog couldn't understand any of the man's words, yet he sensed the kindness the man had extended him. The voice had been soothing and warm, his touch gentle, and when the man left, the dog was gripped with confusion.

The man hopped the fence and ran away, past the trees, past the building where humans came and went. Like the other humans had done before, the man disappeared, leaving the dog alone.

The dog's ears flopped down, his eyes dulled at the thought the man was gone.

The man had looked back at him as he ran, something the dog's owner had not done when the dog had been abandoned, left tied to a tree.

It was different this time, because the dog didn't sense any signs of betrayal in the man's behavior, so the dog stayed where he was, watching, waiting, hoping.

Soon, a man appeared from around the building.

The dog stayed to the shadows as he assessed the

human who walked with purpose.

Sniff, sniff.

It was the man and he had returned with food!

The dog rose and wiggled out from under the barbed wire fence.

"I got you something to eat," the man said. He extended a hand holding half a sandwich. The dog didn't understand the words, but he did understand the offering of food.

With wide eyes and salivating glands in full swing, the dog eagerly took the sandwich and with a gulp he consumed the food. He impatiently waited as the man poured water into a bowl, but before the man had emptied out the water, the dog pushed his way to the bowl and greedily drank.

"I told you I'd be back, that you could trust me." The man stroked the dog's back, long, soothing strokes that comforted the dog.

As the dog lapped water, filling his belly, he didn't notice the man reach behind him, pulling a looped rope out of his pocket.

The dog immediately picked up the scent of hemp, bringing back the memory of being tethered to the tree, but before he could act, the man deftly swung the rope around the dog's neck and pulled once to tighten it.

Instinctively, the dog bristled at the rope. He jerked hard and tried to bolt but the man held on. Struggling against the rope tightening against his neck, the dog thrashed and yelped, shaking his head.

Panic set in.

He barked and snapped, throwing his body on the ground. All the while, the man talked in a soothing voice. The dog panted and hyperventilated, snarling his rage at being tricked.

This went on for a minute or two until the dog tired of the struggle.

With no more fight in him, and weak from the elements, the dog surrendered to the man with the trusting voice.

The man gave a small tug of the rope. "Come on. I'm not going to hurt you."

The dog stood there on wobbly legs, trying to hold firm, afraid to leave. With pleading eyes and a tucked tail the dog looked at the man. One more slight tug on the rope convinced the dog that resisting was futile. Reluctantly, he followed behind, tail tucked. He turned and took one last look at the place he had called home; the place he had come to know the little white dog.

When he reached the truck, the man reached under the dog's belly and helped him into the cab. He retrieved a towel from the back, folded it, and placed in on the seat. He patted it, indicating for the dog to sit on it.

The dog sniffed the towel, smelling the scents left by the man. The man patted it again, finally coaxing the dog over onto the towel.

Gingerly, the dog stepped onto the towel. He lowered his body and pillowed into it.

The man stroked his head, and the dog breathed out deeply as he closed his eyes, savoring the touch of the warm and strong hand.

The dog was helpless and at the mercy of this new man. He hung his head, resting on the towel, eyes weary, unsure of what the future would bring.

Chapter 3

An hour later, Brendon came to the old ranch house, situated on a wide one lane blacktop only a few miles from Bastrop, a small city located in central Texas.

"We're home, boy." Brendon reached to the dog and stroked his head. "I told you I'm with you for the long run. If you don't run away, I won't either. Deal?"

Unsure what to do, the dog remained still.

"We've got a lot to do, and I'm hungry. Let's go on in."

He heaved the duffle bags over his shoulder and let the dog out of the truck. Walking up to the empty house, leash in hand, Brendon thought back to the tragedy at the ranch that had taken place when he was a child. It had been twenty years since the family moved from the ranch in the area of Texas known as the Lost Pines, leaving behind all the unresolved memories and emotions.

Steeling himself, he took a big breath, opened the door, and flipped on a light switch. With it came all the memories and emotions he'd worked hard to suppress. He had to deal with it at some point, and he was glad he had company because he wasn't sure he could handle this on his own.

The dog walked in and sniffed the air. It was stale and smelled of a long-ago smoldering fire. The smoke had seeped into the crevices, filling little spaces new paint or carpet couldn't reach. The dog worried over the unusual smell, like something had perished in the fire. The dog took a few tentative steps and padded over to the kitchen, sniffing along the floorboards, his mind searching for the meaning of the old, smoky odor.

"You know what a kitchen is, don't ya?" Brendon said. "Smart dog. Looking for food? Here you go, boy." Brendon placed a piece of bread and ham on a paper plate. "I'll get you some decent dog food tomorrow. In the meantime, people food will have to do."

The dog inhaled the food as if he wasn't going to eat for a long while, likely behavior he had learned in order to survive at the rest stop Brendon figured.

"What am I going to name you?"

The dog pricked his ears at the rising intonation. He knew the man was talking to him, but the communication between dog and owner was too new for him to understand.

"I think I'll name you Bo in honor of my Beauregard ancestors who lived in Louisiana. You like that name? Huh? Bo?"

There it was again, the same questioning intonation, and the repeated sounds.

Brendon made direct eye contact and Bo returned the communication.

"Your name is Bo. Got it? Bo."

The man came over to Bo and took a handful of fur. He massaged Bo behind the ears, along the scruff of his back while the man repeated the sounds. The touch felt warm and good, and Bo knew then this man would be his. He knew when the man said the particular sound of *Bo*, he should pay attention and learn.

The man was good.

Over the next several days, Brendon and Bo came to know each other.

Brendon learned that Bo liked to be scratched behind

his ears and on his tummy. He didn't like loud noises or being left alone for any length of time. Bo's fur grew back into its former luscious appearance. Bo much preferred to be outside, though Brendon only let him out if he was supervised. He still didn't trust Bo enough to not run away.

One morning, Brendon surveyed the interior of the house, making a mental checklist of the amount of work he needed to do. As he glanced at the boarded up room down the hallway, the signs of the fire were still visible. Brendon couldn't bring himself to go in there. The memories were too much for him to deal with so he turned his attention to the main living area which he could fix.

The white tile countertops and floors were a throwback to the 70s, along with the carpeted den area. Brendon supposed all the cabinets needed were a good cleaning, sanding, some primer, and a new coat of paint. That should be easy enough. Maybe he'd stop at the local bookstore and pick up a couple of home decorating magazines. The house needed a lot of work, and he had no idea what was trendy now.

The decades old carpet would have to go.

Getting an idea, he walked over to the corner of the den, bent down, and dug his fingers into the corner of the carpet. After a bit, he loosened the carpet that had been tacked down, and to his surprise there were hardwoods under the dreadful carpet. He moved the sofa and end tables to the side then pulled the carpet away from the walls. When he was finished, he rolled the carpet and pad up, took them outside, and heaped them on the trash pile.

Walking back into the house, Brendon took a satisfied glance at the result. He took a deep breath, thinking it immediately smelled better in the house. There were nail marks in the hardwoods from where the carpet had been tacked down. He didn't mind it, thinking a little bit of wear and tear was okay. The original floors weren't in bad shape after all. They'd need refinishing, but for the time being they looked quite good.

The only decorations were a few old dusty portraits of long-dead relatives hanging in the upstairs hall, and since he found those to be creepy, he took them down and tucked them away in a closet.

When he moved in, decades of dust covered the few remaining pieces of furniture including a wooden dining table, some chairs, and a chest-of-drawers in the bedroom. He'd opened all the windows and doors and swept the dust out of the house.

There were a few dishes in the cupboards, and some old pots and pans he salvaged, and after a good scrubbing, they were usable.

Regardless of how much he cleaned or tried to stay busy, his thoughts went to the conversation he had with Krishna, his friend and owner of the mini mart where the shooting took place. It was the shooting where Brendon had to discharge his service pistol, leaving a man dead.

One day, two years after the shooting, Krishna had come over to Brendon's apartment in Houston to make him breakfast, and to try to coax him out of his two year self-imprisonment.

Krishna had poured him coffee, and Brendon recalled the conversation with brilliant clarity.

"Tell me what you remember about that day," Krishna said.

"I'd rather not," Brendon said.

"My son, it's part of your healing, and I think it's time. Two years of self-imprisonment is enough." Krishna's voice was fatherly.

Brendon nodded. "I remember walking out of the men's restroom, and was making sure my uniform was tucked in and that my equipment was okay. The sun was blinding and I saw this man standing at the counter pointing a .38 at me. I remember thinking he might have been a strung out junkie, but junkies don't look that good. He had this desperate look on his face, like nothing was going to get in the way of him robbing the store.

"Still, there was something amiss about him. I couldn't quite place it. Next thing I knew something hit me hard in the chest, and I had a hard time catching my breath. The realization hit me that I had been shot. My training kicked in, I brought up my Glock and I aimed at the man at the counter. I think I hit him because he fell down. Things went blurry after that."

"You had been shot twice," Krishna said.

"I remember laying on the floor in something warm and smelling of iron." Brendon looked at Krishna. "It was my blood I was laying in. Right before I passed out, I looked at the man I had killed. His eyes pierced right through me and I swear he mouthed his wife's name."

"Allison."

"Right. Allison is her name." Brendon hung his head. "You know, her young daughter died from cancer the same day her husband did."

"I know. I read it in the papers."

"How much worse can it get for someone?" Brendon took a sip of coffee. "When I wake up, my first conscious thought is of that man I killed. Before I even open my eyes, I see him staring at me. Vacant eyes, staring right through me. Do you how that has affected me? The guilt and shame I've endured?"

Brendon stirred his coffee with a spoon, round and round, clinking the sides, his eyes glazing over. He tapped the coffee from the spoon and set it down. He finished the coffee and swallowed hard.

"I never, ever expected to draw my gun on duty. Do you know what the chances are of a policeman drawing his gun? Or having to fire it? Better yet, killing someone? I thought I'd have a better chance of winning the lottery or being struck by lightning." Brendon got up and took the cup to the kitchen. "Most policemen go through their whole career never once having to draw their gun."

"I'm sorry you had to," Krishna said.

Brendon put both hands on the counter and hung his head, his eyes focused on the cold linoleum squares until they blurred together into a hazy void.

"Do you know what it's done to me? The guilt I've had to live with? Every night right before I try to fall asleep, I see that man staring blankly at me, saying his wife's name. I can't get that out of my head." Brendon looked up at Krishna. "I took that man from his family. He wasn't after money to buy drugs. He needed money to buy medicine for his dying daughter. If I had known that I would have gladly given him money." Brendon swore under his breath. "Why didn't he ask me for help?"

"Brendon," Krishna said with fatherly conviction, "I have no answers, and it doesn't help replaying that in your mind. There is one thing I am certain of: I was there and you had no choice except to use your service pistol to protect yourself. Don't forget you saved my life too. Doesn't that count for something?"

"It does," Brendon admitted. "I've asked myself a hundred million times if I could have done something different."

"You cannot do this," Krishna said. "What happened has happened. It happened for a reason."

"A reason? There's no reason for killing a father that was trying to help his child."

"You didn't know that at the time. Brendon, I am almost old enough to be your father. May I give you some fatherly advice?"

Brendon nodded.

"There are two things you must do. First you need to forgive yourself, because with forgiveness you become stronger. Here," Krishna tapped his head, "and here." He thumped the palm of his hand over his heart. "Your mind and body are connected. When one is healthy, the other is too, and when one is sick, so is the other. If you forgive yourself you will be able to release yourself from your self-imposed imprisonment."

After a long moment, Brendon asked, "What else do I need to do?"

"You need to ask the man's wife for forgiveness."

Brendon said nothing.

"Brendon," Krishna said pointedly, "you need to ask Allison for forgiveness."

"What am I supposed to say?"

"I don't know. When you seek her out and get to know her, and when it is time, the words will come to you and the words will be honest and from the heart. We all make choices in life. Some we make on our own, while some are forced upon us. This is a choice you must make."

At first Brendon scoffed at Krishna's suggestion, but after a long soul-searching session and additional fatherly advice Krishna gave him, Brendon came to understand the wisdom in the request.

It hadn't been hard to find Allison – he only had to do a quick internet search, and when he discovered she had moved to Bastrop and had opened a tailoring and gift shop, his decision to move home was already made for him.

Chapter 4

"Sew Good to See You."

Allison Hartley answered the phone in her usual chipper voice, never tiring of saying the name of the tailor and gift shop she owned near the town square in Bastrop, Texas.

"How can I help you today?" she said, cradling the phone to her ear while holding straight pins in her other hand.

"Allison, good mornin'. It's Lee Mercer."

"Oh, hi, Lee." Her voice was devoid of any inflection. "What can I do for you?" She put the pins down on the table. Multi-tasking was something Allison was efficient at, a balancing act necessary in her fast paced world as a small business owner and single mother.

"I tore my pants again. Ripped a big hole right smack on the side of my pants crawling through a barbed wire fence trying to get to a precious little calf that had gotten separated from its mama."

"Really?" Allison didn't believe him for a moment.

"As a matter of fact, yes. It was the cutest little calf you've ever seen, big eyes–"

"No, not the calf, I'm sure it was cute. I mean, you tore another pair of pants?"

"I've got them to prove it. Can I bring them in to be repaired?"

"Look, Lee, I know you are trying to bring me business, but I'm doing fine without all your ripped pants and shirts. Let me see," Allison said, rummaging through a stack of receipts tucked away in a corner of the counter. "Last week you popped off a button, then the week before that you brought in a pair of pants that had been ripped. Here's one for a pair of pants that were too long, and another one for a suit jacket that needed the cuffs turned up."

There was silence on the other end.

"Need I go on?" Allison asked.

"You got me red handed. I'm clumsy and don't know how to shop."

"If you were married—"

"—which I'm not."

"—I would tell you to save a buck and have your wife make the repairs."

"Allison, you know my wife has been gone for a while now." Lee paused, lowered his voice and said, "God rest her soul."

Allison let out a big sigh. "Okay. Bring them in."

Why had she done that? To tell Lee Mercer to bring in his pants she must be a glutton for punishment, and she mentally chastised herself for feeling sorry for him whenever he brought up the fact he was a recent widower. She wondered why he kept bringing up the subject of his dead wife, then realized she knew the answer to that question. He was trying to make her feel sorry for him. Lee always gave Allison a creepy feeling, studying her like she was some sort of a museum exhibit.

Allison knew Lee wanted to date her and all her efforts to rebuff him or making excuses for not seeing him didn't get through that thick skull of his. It wasn't the age difference that mattered (Lee was twenty years her senior) or the fact he was a widower. Age wouldn't make a difference if the right guy came along.

Plain and simple, it was the way Lee strutted around like he was a big man on campus. And that weird gait of his? Who walked like that? He pranced around like he was a show horse or something.

Her day had been perfect up until his phone call.

She placed the receipts back in the wooden box and tucked it away in a drawer. Finding a duster, she walked over to the front of her store, perusing the shelves, dusting and straightening. Taking a glance at her store, she was satisfied at the inventory she had stocked up on: candles, wicker baskets, T-shirts with homemade emblems, quaint pictures, paintings and photographs from the locals, antique furniture she had refurbished. Always a voracious reader, she educated herself by reading books she checked out at the library and by studying magazines about antique collecting.

With her store doubling as a tailor and tourist shop showcasing refurbished antiques and other irresistible purchases, her income provided a decent living for her and her twelve year old son, Josh.

Allison sensed the time had come for Josh to forge his own identity. Gradually, he was pulling away from her. Minor things at first, like sleeping late and spending more time with his friends, and Allison had caught him looking at girls in the way boys do. She supposed it was the natural way of life—a boy pulling away from his mother and identifying more with his male contemporaries. In times like these Allison desperately wished Doug was here. A boy needed his father, and what was Allison going to do for a male role model for Josh? Certainly not Lee Mercer.

It was too bad Lee had interrupted her day, and what a beautiful day it was, even though it was hot and dry and there wasn't a cloud in the morning sky.

Allison walked over to the thermostat and adjusted the temperature. It was going to be another scorcher.

Her store was located on Main Street in Bastrop, the county seat, located about thirty miles east of Austin in an area known as the "Lost Pines", where a disjunctive population of pine trees thought to be descendants of the great forests of the Ice Age populated the countryside. Walking through those pines was like taking a walk back in time to what the primeval forests must have looked like when rainfall was abundant, not like now with the drought. Even the Colorado River, which cut through the town, was dreadfully low, something the locals were always talking about. Not even the old timers could recall the river being so low.

Thirty minutes later Lee was in Allison's store. He plopped down a new pair of pants on the counter.

"Where are the pants you ripped?" Allison asked.

"Oh, those old things? I threw them out. I bought a new pair and they're a little too long. Can you hem them for me?"

Allison eyed him suspiciously and was about to send him on his way when she had a change of heart. Business was business. Plus, if she charged him double maybe he wouldn't be so eager to come back.

"Alright," she said. "Go change in the back room, and come out when you're done."

A few minutes later Lee waltzed through the curtain like he was making an entrance at the Grand Ole Opry in Nashville, the mirror his adoring audience.

Allison ignored the show. "Step up on the platform and face the mirror." She purposely left off, 'please'.

Lee did as he was told, and that was okay with Lee because it gave him an opportune time to admire his physique in the mirror.

Blake O'Connor

He stood board straight and admired his taut stomach. Working out at the gym five days a week suited him just fine. Those twenty year olds had nothing on this old man. He gave his reflection a once over, eyeing his body like he was checking out a beauty queen with curves in all the right places. He grinned and let out a satisfied breath. Yes, sir, he was looking good, and Lee gave the mirror a 'sup' nod, like he was badass.

Allison was kneeling at the base of the platform, running her long and nimble fingers along Lee's pants, turning them inside out, handling them, fondling them.

Damn, she is a good looking hot little filly, Lee was thinking all the while.

Too bad her hands weren't on something else of his, something that belonged in his pants.

Allison bent over to retrieve an errant pin on the floor, giving Lee a bird's eye view down her loose shirt where he got a glimpse of her cleavage and a pretty little lacy bra.

Allison snapped her head up, staring straight at Lee, whose eyes were firmly planted down the front of her shirt. When she straightened up, Lee quickly averted his eyes, pretending to be looking at a supermodel gracing the cover of magazine on the counter.

"Aren't you a little old for that?" Allison asked.

"To look at a pretty lady?" he replied, pointing to the magazine.

"You know what I mean." Allison crossed her arms and looked at him with narrow eyes.

"No, I don't." Lee scratched the back of his head. "Oh come on, don't give me that look." He tapped the model's picture on the magazine. "All I'm doing is admiring the photograph on the cover."

"Right," Allison said. Uncrossing her arms, she planted her hands on her hips.

"Look, I'm sorry, I'm a guy. I may be a little old, but

34

I'm not dead. I see a pretty lady, I look. What's the harm in looking?" Lee stepped down off the platform and positioned himself closer to Allison. She mirrored the step backwards. "Why don't you let me make it up to you and take you to lunch? We can go to the Kountry Kitchen for their lunch special."

"Lee, I can't. I've got a lot of work to do so it's best we finish. As in n*ow*."

"Okay." His voice was irritated. "I get the message."

After Lee changed and handed the new pants back to Allison, she charged him double for the work, explaining to him it was more difficult to turn up hems than to repair a hole on a worn pair of jeans. Lee told Allison her superb work and attention to detail was worth every penny.

He exultantly strode out of her store. Next he would be clicking his heels together in the air, which he actually did before turning around and taking his hat off followed by a deep bow. Allison rolled her eyes. She propped an elbow on the counter, put her hand to her forehead, and couldn't believe she fell for it.

Lee was becoming a real problem.

He had made his intentions known, a slight brush against her, the way he hung on her every word, the eye contact that lingered a little too long. She rebuffed his continuing overtures, making it known that she wasn't looking for a romantic partner. God, no, because being with someone else would make her feel like she was betraying Doug's memory or being unfaithful.

She felt like she was still married to Doug.

In the two years since the deaths of her husband Doug and daughter Madison, Allison had thrown herself into building a new life for herself and for her son, creating a safe home environment and finding a good school for Josh. With each passing day, Josh looked more like his father, and at times, his uncanny resemblance to Doug comforted her, knowing Doug lived on in his son.

Losing her daughter to cancer was almost unbearable, and it was remarkable Allison hadn't lost her mind.

Lost in thought, Allison's fingers unconsciously went to her neck, feeling the gold chain she wore. She lifted it up, found the locket, and twirled it delicately between her thumb and index finger.

Decorated with a single tiny diamond radiating a sunburst effect, the round, smooth locket gave her peace of mind, calmed her when she was upset or nervous, and never once had she removed the locket she held so close to her heart. An heirloom passed down in her family, first belonging to her great grandmother, who passed it down until it became Allison's. She had intended to pass it to Madison, and the thought that she didn't have a daughter to pass it to made her sad.

Allison had promised Madison she would wear the necklace with the starburst locket with Madison's picture inside. Family lore said it was supposed to have good luck powers. Allison intended to keep the promise, irrespective of circumstances or whether she was a hundred years old.

Maybe a little luck would come her way.

Chapter 5

It was early June, and it was hot. The air-conditioner whirled and sputtered, trying to keep Allison's store cool. The east sun beamed through the plate glass windows, making the area near the front even hotter.

Being a single mother of twelve year old Josh had its ups and downs, and she was thankful for the social security money provided to her since Doug had died. She didn't like to think about that time, and how Doug had been killed in the robbery of the mini mart.

The questions Josh asked about his father bothered Allison the most, and it behooved her to lie to Josh about how his father died. Still considering him a child, she protected Josh the best she could.

When the time was right, she would tell him the truth before someone else did. As it was, she had told him Doug had suffered a heart attack and died instantly.

She couldn't bring herself to tell Josh the family was almost destitute because Doug had been unemployed for months. They needed money to pay for Madison's medicine, and because his father was so desperate to help Madison that he had committed armed robbery, dying during it, and had almost killed a police officer. She couldn't do that to the memory of Doug. It was best that Josh didn't know. He was at such a delicate age with so many physical and psychological changes thrust upon him.

Only Allison's best friend, Susan Harrigan, knew the tragic circumstances surrounding Doug's death. She knew Susan would never betray her confidence.

During the days after the shooting, Allison had purposely refrained from watching TV or reading any of the Houston newspapers. She did not want to see his picture or know the name of the man responsible, only referring to him as *that man*. That was how Allison referred to the police officer in her mind when she thought about him. Fortunately or unfortunately depending on how you looked at it, Doug's death had happened during late summer when Josh was out of school. Allison had deliberately kept him from seeing his friends, and right before school started she'd moved to Bastrop, far away from the memories and *that man*.

As far as she was concerned, he didn't even deserve the respect to be called by his name. Others had tried to tell her, to keep her informed of how *that man* had dropped out of society, how he was a distinguished police officer, how no charges were brought against him, yet she did not care one iota what happened to him.

He could rot for all she cared.

Chapter 6

Brendon was getting more nervous by the second.

He had been sitting in his truck for the past thirty minutes trying to get up the nerve to walk into Allison Hartley's shop. The truck was parked at an angle two spaces down from Sew Good to See You.

He fidgeted compulsively, drumming his thumbs on the steering wheel, tapping his foot, scratching his head and his beard when he realized he hadn't shaved this morning. He checked his reflection in the rearview mirror, inspecting the stubble on his face. Okay, maybe he looked a little scruffy. It wasn't too bad. He really needed to calm down or he might blurt something out by accident.

Bo picked up on Brendon's nervousness, which made Bo nervous. Hot dog breath filled the cab of the truck, so Brendon turned up the AC to high.

When his mind was idle Brendon started to recall the shooting, that he had almost died, and would have, if it wasn't for the quick actions of Krishna, owner of the mini mart and Brendon's friend.

One of the bullets had entered his chest and lodged within millimeters of his spine, and the doctors told him he had been really lucky because if it had been any closer he would have been a goner. He had lost a lot of blood, had a collapsed lung, and had been in a medically induced coma for two weeks while his body healed.

He had fuzzy memories of the blinding morning light, of discharging his firearm, Krishna standing over him, calling 911, being whisked away in an ambulance, sirens screaming. He wished he could forget the look of haunting desperation in the dead man's eyes, but he couldn't.

The passage of time had softened the feelings of self-loathing, and after taking Krishna's advice, he only had one more item to check off his list. He had to ask Allison Hartley her for forgiveness.

After that, maybe he could get on with his life. Krishna was right. Two years of self-imposed imprisonment was enough.

Today, Brendon was a different man and he tried not to think about the man he'd killed at the mini mart. Sometimes it was useless to resist. Lately, though, he felt better, even thinking he would have purpose to his life once he talked to Allison.

Surely, she'd forgive him. It might be a shock at first for her to meet the man responsible for her husband's death. However, once she got to know him, she'd realize he was a good man.

Brendon had served his community by being a policeman, did an honest day's work, and had honorably stayed by his parents' side until their deaths. Wasn't that what a good son did? Didn't a good son become a good man?

Brendon clasped his fingers together, stretched his arms out in front of him, and cracked his knuckles.

A loud *woof* snapped him out of his trance.

In the weeks they had been together, Bo didn't leave Brendon's side. They had been together 24/7, working, eating, and sleeping together. Well, maybe not in the same bed, rather in the same room. Brendon had made Bo a pallet to sleep on next to the bed.

They were still getting to know each other, their likes and dislikes, though Bo had already learned the commands Brendon gave him, like *sit, wait, let's go, time to eat*, simple things like that. Bo possessed a superb ability to gauge his owner's emotions, and sitting in the truck, Bo was aware of his owner's nervousness.

Bo sidled up to Brendon, nosing his arm.

"You think it's time we go in?" Brendon looked at Bo, who canted his head and pricked his ears.

"That's what I thought, too. Let's go."

Understanding the command, Bo rose and wiggled from side to side, eager to get out of the truck.

Just when Brendon got the nerve to get out of his truck, someone walked into the store. Some guy, about 55 or so, didn't much look like a rancher or businessman. He had a pair of pants draped over his arm, so he must have been one of her customers.

For a while, Brendon sat in his truck, observing Allison and her customer. Even though he couldn't hear their conversation, he guessed there was tension between the two judging by her body language. When the guy admired himself in the mirror while Allison was fiddling with the trouser hem, Brendon thought, *What a loser.*

To top it off, he caught the guy looking down Allison's shirt. That was for teenage boys, not a grown man. Brendon wanted to get out right then and show that guy a thing or two, like how to show a lady some respect.

He reached over to the glove compartment and retrieved the piece of paper he had printed so long ago. It had become jagged at the edges from being folded and refolded so many times, and he had to tape them back together so the paper wouldn't fall apart. Unfolding it for the umpteenth time, he looked at Allison's picture. So many times he'd imagined what he would say to her, how he would introduce himself. The things she would say to him, how she'd flash that megawatt smile at him.

He felt like he already knew Allison before they even spoke their first words to each other.

What was he going to say to her? *Hi, I'm Brendon McMahon, the policeman who shot your husband.*

Like that would be a good way to get to know a person. Wrong.

What kind of excuse could he make up for stopping by her store?

He wasn't a tourist, so that wouldn't fly. If he had planned better, he would have brought in a pair of pants than needed hemming. She *was* a tailor after all.

Brendon checked the time.

The men's clothing store he passed on the way here should be open by now. It would only take him a few minutes to run in and buy a pair of pants. By the time he got back that loser of a guy should have left her store. That plan sounded good and actually doing something would get his mind off of what he was about to do. He tore out of the parking space, gunned the engine, and in no time flat he had already checked out of the store and was back in the same parking space.

Brendon was about to cut the engine when he noticed Loser Guy still in the store.

Trying to divert his attention, Brendon kept changing the channels on the radio, groaning that all the local stations were country. Not because he didn't like country, rather, he had never paid much attention to the lyrics. Now that he was trying to get his mind off of the reason he was here, he listened intently to the lyrics. Those songs were so sad, someone always singing about lost love or their wife that had died, or longing to be young.

Enough sadness, so he changed the channel to a sports talk radio show, where the announcer talked endlessly about the same subject Brendon had little interest in.

Back to country music.

Finally the guy left. When he did a little happy dance, Brendon couldn't help to think not only was the guy a loser, he was also a jerk.

He decided to wait a couple more minutes so he could compose himself and get up the nerve to walk into her store. Wouldn't you know it? He waited too long. She got another customer, this time an attractive middle-aged woman, and by the looks of it, they were friends.

He checked his watch, changed channels again, ran his fingers through his hair, and adjusted the AC a little. He couldn't control his sweating. Twenty long minutes of more waiting tortured him. He'd had it waiting around, so he cut the engine, opened the truck door and decided it was now or never.

Chapter 7

Allison had watched Lee until he was completely out of sight. She could relax a little now. It was then she realized her shoulders were almost up to her ears. She dropped her shoulders, rolled them, and exhaled a cleansing breath.

The store was quiet and her thoughts harkened back to Doug and Madison and what her daughter had said before she died: *Look to the stars*. Allison repeated the phrase over and over, wondering what it meant.

She stayed busy running a business, and being a single mom didn't allow her much time for anything else. Her lifestyle didn't allow her time to date, or to even consider remarrying, because she was not ready to become involved in a relationship. Dating different men would have confused Josh, and suppose the relationship ended badly, or if Josh became too attached to someone? She wouldn't put him through losing anybody else.

Or was it that she didn't want to put *herself* through losing another husband? It was something she didn't want to think about.

The grief of Doug and Madison's deaths was something Allison worked hard to overcome. Doug had been the love of her life, and she imagined growing old with him, retiring and traveling like they had always talked about. Those plans had been derailed. In fact, her whole life had jumped the tracks. Losing a child to cancer had almost made her go crazy, and if it hadn't been for her son Josh, Allison thought she might have curled up and died so she could be reunited with her husband and daughter.

She was a fighter though, and each day got a little easier. She could hear Doug's strong voice and sage advice: *When things get tough, take it an hour at a time, and if that's too much, then five minutes at a time.* Sometimes making it through an hour seemed like a colossal amount of time, something so insurmountable she could only think about the next five minutes.

She had a renewed purpose in life with her store, raising Josh, and in reality, she could remarry, and maybe the time had come for her to revisit the issue. Thinking of Lee gave her the creeps. Lately, though, she had sensed a change in him. Perhaps it was because he was lonely and needed something to occupy his time, and he did have an inordinate amount of pants and shirts that were missing a button, or had broken zippers. He was becoming more possessive of her, making excuses to see her, and Allison dreaded him coming into the store.

While she jotted down notes in her appointment calendar, she stole a glance out the windows of her shop. The dry season was in full swing with low humidity and cloudless skies that stretched as far as the eye could see. The land sorely needed a good rain, especially with the year-long Biblical drought.

Allison finished her notes and turned around when the bells on the front door chimed, announcing a customer.

She put on her *hi-can-I-help-you-face*, not something that was hard for her to do because she genuinely liked helping people. She immediately relaxed when her best friend Susan Harrigan, the owner of Susan's Bed & Breakfast, stepped through the door carrying two cups of coffee, a few posters tucked under her arms, and all the latest gossip she couldn't wait to share with Allison.

The door rattled shut, the bells jingled, and the window panes jiggled from the gentle vibrations.

"Whew, it's gonna be another scorcher," Susan said. She put the coffee on the counter and set down the posters. "Why is it that we still drink hot coffee in this heat?" she asked not expecting an answer. She picked up a magazine and fanned her face. "Jesus, it's only ten in the morning and it must be eighty-five effing degrees." She fanned her blouse and stepped over to where a vent blew cool air onto her neck and down her shirt. "Ah. That feels better already. It's nice and cool in here."

"I keep it that way because customers don't like to sweat when trying on clothes," Allison said.

"Heck, maybe I'll close up my bed and breakfast and learn how to sew."

"You can't even thread a needle, Susan," Allison reminded her. "If you're hot, why don't you put some ice in the coffee?"

"Don't mind if I do." Susan looked around. "Where's the ice?"

"In the back."

"Want me to get you some too?"

"No thanks. I like my coffee hot and strong."

"Hmm, a metaphor for the kind of man you want," Susan said wryly, arching an eyebrow.

"Don't start. Okay? I'm not looking for a man."

"I know, Allie, but that's when you'll find one!"

"Really? Like I haven't heard *that* before. I'm not looking for a man. I've got my hands full with the shop and raising Josh. It doesn't leave me any time for myself."

"You don't have to convince me, only yourself. You know, Allie, I've seen the way Lee looks at you. He'd be an okay catch, no baggage, kids grown. Plus, he came out a richer man after his wife died. Talk is that he took out a million dollar policy on her a year before she died."

"That's gossip. How do you know that?"

"Brian is friends with the local insurance guy. He was sworn to secrecy, and if it was meant to be a secret he wouldn't have told anyone in the first place. Oh, who cares anyway? You'd never have to worry about supporting yourself or paying that mortgage you took out on your house and land."

"Susan," Allie said in exasperation, shaking her head, "I'm managing quite well. Things are a little tight. It's nothing I can't handle. Let me remind you, Lee is only a friend."

"A friend with benefits?" Susan asked before turning to head to the back where she ducked through the curtains leading to the storage room.

"No!" Allison shouted. "Definitely no benefits."

Moments later Susan emerged with a large Styrofoam cup full of ice. She dropped a few cubes into a smaller cup and poured the hot coffee over the ice. She took a sip, sucked in a melting ice cube, swirling it around in her mouth before crunching it.

"You know what they say when you crunch ice?" Allison asked, teasing her friend.

"What?"

"That you're sexually frustrated."

"Then by all means let me get you a bucket of ice!" Susan chimed in, offering up the large cup, filled to the brim with ice cubes.

Allison laughed heartily. "Good comeback!"

"It's so good to hear you laugh, Allie. You're young, beautiful, skinny, and you've got blonde hair that doesn't come from a bottle. There must be a million men looking for someone like you. You shouldn't be alone."

"I'm not alone. I have Josh."

"You know what I mean," Susan said. "You're

hopeless." She picked up a magazine and started flipping through the pages, uninterested in reading any of the articles.

Allison took a sip of coffee before stepping over to the industrial sewing machine, and with a couple of pins balanced precariously between her lips she placed the man's jacket sleeve on the flat end of the table. She removed the pins and stuck them in a pin cushion. Using a seam ripper, she carefully pried open the seam stitch by stitch until the lining was exposed, careful not to brush off the white chalky markings she had made earlier during a fitting.

"It's been a long time since anyone called me 'Allie'."

"Who used to call you that?" Susan asked.

"Doug."

"Oh, I'm sorry. I didn't mean to bring up bad memories. If you'd rather, I won't call you that anymore. You're my best friend and I don't want to do anything to upset you."

"You didn't upset me. I want you to call me 'Allie'. It was Doug's pet name for me, and I like thinking about him, hearing his voice. It's okay to say his name, to remind me of him." Allison sat back in the chair and looked out the window. "Sometimes I imagine the only reason he isn't here is because he's on a long trip, vacationing somewhere warm and sunny. Perhaps he went to the Caribbean where the water is blue and the sand is white. Whenever someone opens the door to my shop and the bells jingle, I look up and for a moment, a brief moment, I hope it's him. Don't ever say you're sorry for mentioning his name or say it with regret. We had ten wonderful years together and his memory keeps me going. He wouldn't want me to be sad at the thought of him. Hearing his name keeps him alive in my heart, reminds me of Madison and all our happy times together."

"He was the love of your life, wasn't he?" Susan asked.

"Yes, he was."

"Think you'll ever marry again?"

"I don't know. Doug was my Mr. Right, and unless another Mr. Right magically happens to walk through the front door, it will be a long time before I marry again."

Chapter 8

For a while it was silent in the store. Low background noise from an early morning TV news channel filled the shop with meaningless chatter. Lumbering tourists strolled on the sidewalk, perusing locally made wares. The sun streamed through the windows, and the man in the truck continued to observe.

"Where's the remote?" Susan asked. "I think the weather forecast is next. I want to hear what the forecaster has to say. There might be a chance of rain."

Allison titled her head, motioning to the coffee table. "It should be there somewhere. Look under the magazines."

Susan rummaged around through the magazines. "Found it." Picking it up, she clicked through the channels until she found the station she wanted. "What's up with these female weathermen? Or is it politically correct to say 'weather person' now? Have you noticed how all of them are really young and bleached blonde, and wear a dress size too small? Do you think it's mandated in their contract to wear such tight clothes?" She squinted at the TV. "If that dress is any tighter, a button might fly right off and smack one of the cameramen upside their heads!"

Allison glanced at the TV. "Haven't you heard?" she deadpanned. "Flying buttons are the number one killer of cameramen."

Susan harrumphed.

Allison laughed. "Those sisters *are* about to bust out!" She put down the pants she was working on and looked at Susan. "It's a distraction so that the guys won't care if the forecast is wrong."

A map of the southwestern part of the United States filled the TV screen, with circular red lines indicating the immense high pressure system that had settled in over Texas. Susan knew what that meant: No rain in the near future.

"Damn! Can't we get a little rain?" Susan asked. She pressed the mute button. "Maybe a drop? Is that too much to ask? We already lost some really big shade trees last year."

"What about the cattle at your place?" Allison asked.

"Brian has been using hay that he stored last year because there's not enough grass for them."

"How is that husband of yours, anyway?"

Susan shut the magazine she was reading and placed it on a coffee table. "Brian's great, you know him, the stalwart rancher of Bastrop County. He *is* worried about all the pine trees here. They are getting dry, and some have already died along the road to our place. The county doesn't have enough money to clean them out, a burn ban is in effect, and there is always some local yokel that still wants to burn brush. So foolish. The timber is dreadfully dry, and one careless flick of a match or a cigarette and this place will go up in flames."

"All we need is a good tropical storm to blow our way, dump about five inches of a good, soaking rain on us, and our troubles will be over," Allison said. She lifted her gaze and peered out through the glass front panel of her store. "Don't you love storms? There's nothing better than a rainy Sunday morning, listening to the rain on the roof and the trees swaying. Sleeping late, window

51

shades pulled low. Covers pulled up around my chin, all warm and snuggly in my bed. It's like time stands still. Like I'm in a protective cocoon, loving and warm, wrapping me in the moment. Just me and my thoughts with the things I love all around me." Allison paused, turned around and looked at Susan. "Sometimes I wish time would stand still."

"Well, aren't you the poet?"

"Not really." Allison blushed. "But that is my perfect morning."

"Almost perfect," Susan said. "You left out one thing."

"What?"

"You'll figure it out when you have a man," Susan said, reaching for the magazine she had earlier put down. "I do like the part about time standing still. I wish time would stop my wrinkles, but it won't." Susan stretched the sides of her face with her fingers and turned to look at herself in the floor to ceiling mirror. "Are you going to the county fair next month?"

"The July fourth celebration, right?" Allison asked. "Lee wants to see me at the fair. At first I was excited about the fair. Now I'm dreading it. I don't really know what to do about Lee."

"What do you mean?"

"He's been coming to the shop more often with torn pants or a missing button. I know he's looking for an excuse to see me. There is absolutely no spark between us. When Doug and I first met, you could have lit up New York City with the electricity between us. I don't have anything like that with Lee."

"Have you tried?"

"Actually, I have."

"Some guys don't get it. I think with Lee you'll have to spell it out in black and white. Lee's too dense to understand anything else."

"I suppose so. Josh wants to go to the fair, so I'll

probably go. Susan, I worry about Josh and what to do for after school care in the fall. He's getting to that age where he is starting to assert some independence and he thinks he is old enough to stay home alone."

"How old is he?"

"Twelve. He keeps badgering me to let him ride the bus home after school. He's tired of the school's aftercare program, and frankly, he *is* getting a little old for that. I worry about him being by himself. What's he going to do until I get home? What would he do if there was an emergency? Or if he was sick..."

"Allison, stop it," Susan said. She thumped a magazine on the coffee table. "You're a worry wart. Nothing's going to happen. He'll probably watch TV or play video games. For heaven's sake, the boy is twelve. No self-respecting twelve year old would be caught dead in an afterschool program. Don't baby him. Let him grow up."

"It's so hard. I wish he'd stay little forever."

"Like puppies?"

"Exactly. These are the times I really miss Doug. Josh is getting to the age where he needs a male role model and there are some things a mom can't do for her son, like teaching him how to shave, or how to ask out a girl."

"Have him text a girl to ask her out. That's what all the kids do nowadays. Talking on the phone is so last generation."

"He still needs a male role model."

"Lee could help out."

"Never."

"Unless Mr. Perfect walks into your life, Lee may have to do."

"I'm not going to settle."

"You're right. You shouldn't have to," Susan said. "Enough talk about Lee. Getting back to Josh, if he wants to, he can work at my place after school. This month, he has worked almost all day, and besides, he does a really good job. Customers love him and for a child his age, he has great manners and a maturity that most twelve year olds are incapable of. You've done a good job raising him."

"Thanks, Susan. He is a good kid. I don't want him working his childhood away. I think working in the summer at your bed and breakfast is enough. He'll have after school soccer practice several days a week, so that will keep him busy."

"By the way," Susan said, "the civic association wants us to put posters up on the front doors of our shops to advertise the county fair. It's a good way to promote it and hopefully get some return business from the tourists."

"If you don't mind, could you tape some up for me?" Allison asked. "I promised my customer I'd have his jacket ready by noon, after that I'm going to close shop early and head home. I'm going to enjoy every bit of my Saturday afternoon and Sunday, as long as Lee doesn't see me sneak out of here. He asked me to lunch, but I told him I couldn't go."

"Good luck with that. Lee has eyes in the back of his head. Well, break time is over," Susan said. Rising from the sofa, she set the magazine down and stretched. "Where's the tape dispenser?"

"Behind the counter in the top drawer," Allison said. "Do you know if they are planning anything new this year for the 4th of July fair, other than the usual watermelon eating contest?"

"They've hired some local musicians and I've heard that Lee will be the lead singer," Susan said. She peeled off several lengths of tape. She reached up and placed a poster on the window, taping it in place.

"Lee already told me about him singing. I don't need

him crooning for me after what I have planned."

"Oh, what's that?" Susan asked.

"I plan on telling him to find another tailor because I don't want to see him anymore."

"Kinda harsh isn't it?"

"No. Lee is becoming a problem. If Lee was the last man on Earth, and I was the last woman, the human race would become extinct."

"Well, I gotta run," Susan said. She handed the tape dispenser and leftover posters over to Alison. "Back to work. We'll chit-chat later about that guy you're going to meet."

"You're incorrigible." Allison laughed. "I love you anyway. Have a good rest of the day."

When Susan went to push open the door, it swung out instead, and she nearly lost her balance. "Why thank you," she said to the man walking in. She gave him a satisfied onceover. Turning around she half-whispered, half-yelled, "Allison you have a new customer."

Chapter 9

For the past torturous thirty minutes or so, Brendon had been sitting in his pickup, parked two spaces down from Allison's shop. His hands had flitted from the steering wheel, down to his lap, then back up to his hair, he palmed his thighs rubbing them, he adjusted the AC for the fifth unneeded time, scratched his nose then huffed several times before finally being still.

Would she recognize him from his picture that had been splashed all over the front page of the *Houston Chronicle* and from being the main story night after night on all three local TV stations? Killing a man who was only trying to save his child made for sensational TV coverage. Reporters camped out on the hospital doorstep 24/7, giving hourly updates on his progress. When he finally emerged a couple of weeks later battered and bruised, looking like a war survivor, a throng of vipers with TV cameras rushed at him shoving microphones in his face asking, "Sir, do you have any comment on the shooting?" or, "Is there anything you'd like to say to his widow?" And his favorite, "How do you feel about killing a family man?"

Sitting in his truck, he couldn't wait anymore. He had worked up the courage to talk to her, to tell her who he was, and why he had tracked her down.

Abruptly, he killed the engine, shut and locked his

truck, told Bo, "Come on," and bounded up the sidewalk and into Sew Good to See You, almost barreling over the woman walking out. She was about as surprised to see him as he her.

"Nice dog," she had said, or something like that.

While he kept one hand on the door to keep it open, he looked down at the floor before stealing a few nervous glances at the store's interior. It could have been straight out of one of those HGTV shows, what with all the homemade wares and paintings, and furniture draped with quilts. Scented vanilla candles filled the air. A vase full of neatly arranged purple flowers caught his eyes.

A good policeman was always aware of their surroundings.

His heart pounded more the moment he saw her, and all sorts of thoughts crossed his mind: Would she recognize him? If she did, would she throw him out? Would he get down on his knees begging her to listen to him?

"Are dogs allowed?" Brendon blurted out.

"I guess so." Allison glanced at Bo. "Does he mind you?"

"He does." Brendon gave a slight jerk of the leash which got Bo's attention. The dog looked up, waiting for instruction. "Sit."

Bo sat on his haunches.

"He minds."

"Please, come on in."

Brendon walked into Sew Good to See You, unsure what to expect. His heart was pounding so hard he was sure Allison could see it thumping under his shirt.

Bo picked up on Brendon's apprehension so stayed right by his side, walking in step.

To top it off, Brendon had almost flattened the lady walking out. He automatically said, "Excuse me", then fumbled over the next words. At the moment, he couldn't recall exactly what he had said. Hopefully, he hadn't made a fool of himself.

He didn't even hear the doors jingle shut. He just stood there, awestruck at how beautiful Allison was in person. The grainy picture he had of her didn't do her justice. He could stare down the gun-brandishing gang-bangers of the Fifth Ward in Houston, run half a mile and slap handcuffs on a robber without breaking a sweat. Now that he was face to face with her, he could feel the sweat trickling down the side of his face.

After all the rehearsing, and going over every possible scenario, he had absolutely no idea what to say.

For a man who found conversation easy, he was as tongue tied as a tangled ball of string, and hadn't been this nervous since he asked out pretty little Suzy Callahan and her mouthful of braces to the seventh grade dance. When she had said yes to his invitation, it almost gave him a heart attack.

If his heart didn't settle down now, he might have a *real* heart attack.

From the way she looked at him she didn't recognize him.

Good.

Maybe this might work after all.

Chapter 10

Allison quickly sized up her new customer. He was about six feet tall, boyish face, early thirties. Lanky too. Obviously by his tan, he had been working outdoors. Nice, loose fitting faded jeans. His short sleeved shirt revealed muscled arms. Brown tussled hair, a little long perhaps, interspersed with a touch of gray hair.

Much too young for gray hair, she thought. Allison supposed that happened sometimes. She should know about getting gray hairs too soon, but she catalogued those bad memories to the back of her mind. She immediately put on her best store smile, a wide, crinkling, inviting smile. Her heart fluttered and she was surprised at her reaction.

"Good afternoon," Allison said. "Welcome to my store."

"Afternoon." Brendon removed his baseball cap. He closed the glass-paneled door, the beveling catching the sunlight sparkling on the walls. When the door engaged the frame, the bells jingled.

"What can I do for you?" Allison asked.

"I bought a pair of jeans the other day without trying them on because I was in a hurry." He purposely fibbed about when he bought the jeans. He didn't want Allison to know he had bought them a few minutes earlier. "Wouldn't you know it, when I tried them on at home, they were too long. I guess I bought the wrong length. Either that or the jeans were mismarked. Can you take them up?" Brendon held his breath waiting for her to answer.

"You could return them for the correct size."

"Oh, right." He exhaled and raked a hand through his hair. "It's too much trouble, and when I found your shop, well, what do you know? I'm here."

"That you are," Allison said. She extended her arm to Brendon.

Brendon wasn't quite sure what she wanted, so he shook her hand.

"Oh, right. It's nice to meet you." Allison smiled demurely. When her hand was in his, she was overcome by an immediate longing, something she wasn't even aware existed, like a schoolgirl accidentally brushing against the boy she had a crush on. She looked him straight in the eyes and she liked what she saw. She wasn't even aware of how long they had been shaking hands.

"The bag?" he said, still holding her hand.

"Hmm?"

"The bag? Do you need to look at the jeans?"

"Oh, of course." Allison awkwardly withdrew her hand.

Brendon handed the plastic sack to Allison and she took the jeans out, setting them on the counter. When she glanced at the receipt, Brendon noticed the edges of her mouth turn up ever so slightly before relaxing.

"Do you want to keep the receipt?" Allison asked. She didn't plan on telling him she knew he had just bought the pants. Perhaps he bought another pair another time, mixing them up. Men were like that when it came to shopping.

"Yeah, sure," Brendon said.

Allison handed the receipt back to Brendon. "Once I

start cutting on them, you won't be able to return them. Is that okay?"

"Absolutely."

"You're the second customer I've had this morning who bought pants that were too long."

"Men are lousy shoppers. I guess it's good for business."

"I do have my fair share of hemming to do."

Allison walked behind the counter, positioned the pants on the flat surface, and snipped the tags off. She was conscious of the fact he was watching her, and even though the TV was on she became aware of how quiet it was in the store. She sensed that it was making both of them uncomfortable.

"Nice dog you have. What's his name?"

"Bo."

"How long have you had him?"

"About a month."

"That's all? I thought maybe you'd had him for a long time by how well he acts."

"Oh, no. I found him at a rest stop. He was extremely thin, and I felt some sort of immediate connection with him. And him with me. I couldn't leave him there, so I took him with me. I'm still trying to fatten him up, which shouldn't take long because he has a hearty appetite."

"That's so nice you saved him," Allison said. "Sorry, I forgot to introduce myself. I'm Allison Hartley."

"Brendon McMahon." He held his breath, waiting for the tirade that was sure to follow. When there was none, he glanced around the store, trying to think of something clever to say, and when he couldn't he asked, "How long have you been here?"

"A little less than two years. And you?" she asked, looking up at him. When her eyes met Brendon's, she held his gaze for an uncomfortable moment then looked back to the jeans. She touched her face, hoping he wouldn't notice the rosiness filling her cheeks. She puckered her lips and blew cool air onto her chin. She turned, pretending to look for something on the back counter, stalling for time for her cheeks to turn back to a normal color.

"About a month."

"What brought you here?" she asked, her back still turned to him.

He stole a quick peek at her hair, her shoulders, down her back and to her legs.

"Hmm?"

"What brought you here?" Allison asked again.

Brendon shuffled his feet and scratched the stubble on his chin. "I'm actually from here. I inherited some land from my parents that has an old farmhouse on it. It's got some damage from a fire a long time ago, and hasn't been occupied for a long time. I'm trying to fix it."

"To resell?"

"Oh no, I plan on staying."

"Welcome to Bastrop. I think you'll like it here." Allison absentmindedly twirled her necklace.

Brendon noticed the movement. "That's a nice necklace you have."

"Oh, this," she said, holding the locket. She smiled ruefully. "It's a picture of my daughter."

"How old is she?" Brendon asked. When Allison didn't answer immediately, he said, "Sorry, it's none of my business. I didn't mean to pry."

She waved him off. "It's a perfectly normal question. Madison would have been six. She died two years ago from cancer."

Brendon had to think quickly and he didn't like lying because he already knew her daughter had died from cancer. "Oh, I'm terribly sorry. I didn't mean to–"

"It's okay. I keep her picture here in this locket,"

Allison said. She held it away from her décolletage. "I made a promise to her that I would never take it off. Would you like to see her picture?"

"Sure," Brendon said.

Allison leaned over the counter and showed him the locket.

"It has a beautiful star on it."

"My daughter liked stars," Allison said. *Look to the stars*, Madison had said. She opened the locket, inviting Brendon to look at it.

"She's beautiful. She looks just like you."

"Thank you," Allison said. She snapped the locket shut.

A brief silence followed until Brendon asked, "The pants? Will you be able to hem them?"

"Absolutely. I need to get your measurements so I can have them ready for you on Monday. Will that be alright?"

"Yes, of course. I thought it would take longer."

"I work fast, been sewing all my life." She rummaged around the counter looking for the store pad with the number order on it. "All I need is for you to write your name and phone number here," Allison said. She handed him a notepad and a pencil."

While Brendon scribbled his name and number on the pad, Allison looked at him, thinking there was something familiar about him, or about his face or the way he talked, or the way he looked at her. Almost like he knew her.

Brendon handed the note to her.

"Do I know you?" Allison asked.

The question caught Brendon off guard. Did she recognize him from his picture in the Houston paper? He thought quickly. "Don't think so. I always remember the beautiful women I meet."

Allison blushed again.

"See you Monday," Brendon said, heading to the front door, Bo right behind him. He opened it wide and tipped his hat to the woman entering the store. "Excuse me, ma'am," he said, holding the door open.

"Excuse *me*," Susan said. She looked the tall man up and down and watched him and his dog stroll out of the store.

"Susan, what are you doing back here? You just left."

"You know why I'm back here."

"No, I don't."

"Oh no," Allison said. She hurried to the door, holding Brendon's jeans. By the time she got there, Brendon had already backed out of the parking space and was halfway down the street.

"I forgot to take his measurements," Allison said.

"Love struck, already?"

"What? No. He's a customer."

"Seriously? Come on, who is he? What happened?" Susan asked. Her eyes were big and she was almost breathless. "What's his dog's name?"

"Bo."

"Good start. Now give me all the details and don't leave out anything like what color his eyes are. Where is he from? Is he married? Is he wearing a wedding ring? What is he doing here?" Susan plopped down in the sofa and threw her arms over the back of the sofa. "Well?" Susan asked.

"What?"

"Don't play coy with me."

"Oh, give me a break," Allison complained. She folded his jeans and placed them on the counter. "He's a new customer. That's all."

"What about his dog? How long has he had him?"

"Not long. Brendon found the dog at a rest stop."

"You're using his name? That's good."

Allison rolled her eyes.

"So let me get this straight. A tall, good looking, eligible bachelor with a dog *who he saved*, waltzes in here and you tell me not to play coy? Oh, come on," Susan whined.

"He brought in a pair of jeans and asked me if I could take them up. That's all."

"Well, haven't we heard that excuse before!"

"Geez, Susan. I don't even know him."

"Not yet. But you will know him. You'll see."

Reluctant to continue the line of conversation, Allison changed the subject. They talked for a while about inconsequential things like what Susan was making for dinner that night, and the conversation that she and her husband had over breakfast. They talked about the things that best friends can talk about for hours without really saying much of anything. There were movies to discuss, and the latest gossip about whether or not the lead actor was cheating on his wife. All the tabloids said he was.

"Break's over," Susan said. "Back to work."

"Okay, see you later."

The doors to the store jingled shut and Allison was left alone in her shop. Standing at the counter, she put her elbows on the counter, cupping her chin in the palm on her hand. She mused about the man who had walked into her store, Brendon, he'd said, and she replayed everything he had said to her, even the horrified look on his face when he almost ran over Susan. Allison had to admit, he was the most gorgeous man she had seen in a long time. Plus he had manners, and he *had* saved a dog. She felt an immediate attraction to him, and she believed he had the same toward her, or was it the loneliness she had been feeling where she might misinterpret his questions, or interest? It appeared he had a genuine interest in her, even apologizing when he asked her about the necklace. He couldn't know about her daughter, so it had been an innocent question.

Allison pondered one of Susan's questions.

Blue.

His eyes are blue.

Chapter 11

Lee Mercer prided himself on keeping in shape.

If there was only one thing he had learned in the Marines, it was to stay fit. Lee made it a daily practice to do chin-ups, push-ups, and he ran five miles every day, come hell or high water. There was none of the latter, and for the past several months he had been running in god awful heat. Along with his exercise regimen, the ranch work kept his upper body in shape for hauling hay bales and hundred pound feed sacks. It wasn't for the weak of body or mind, both of which Lee thought he excelled in.

He thumbed his nose at others his age who had become paunchy and soft around the middle from lack of exercise and years of indulging in too many sweets and carbs, or imbibing on too many high caloric cocktails.

It was Sunday morning and Lee stepped out of the shower and walked over to the bathroom sink of his ranch house, where he stood butt naked and washboard straight. He flexed his muscles in a gorilla stance like he was trying out for an Iron Man contest.

Fifty-five years old. Not too shabby at all.

Taking a hand towel, he briskly rubbed his Marine-style cropped hair, inspected the amount of gray that was becoming more evident, deciding he needed a little tune-up. He read the directions on the hair dye package, and like it instructed, smeared a dab of petroleum jelly to the sides of his hair where a little gray would look natural. He was careful not to dye all his hair, because that would have looked fake, and Lee didn't like fake people.

He might have numerous personality flaws, but being a hypocrite wasn't one of them.

He waited the allotted time for the hair dye to remain on his hair before washing it out. Coming out his hair, it had just the right amount of gray left, and he thought he looked a little like Sean Connery. He was cocky, too, and tall like the old Scot who swaggered around in those vintage James Bond movies. Men should be men, and women should be women. It took his thoughts to Allison Hartley.

Man, what was wrong with her?

Lee had practically bent over backwards when she first moved to Bastrop, helping her unload a heavy piece of furniture along with the gazillion boxes on that hot day. Wasn't that altruistic of him to take time out of his busy day to help a lady in need? *He* thought so. He had been driving down the county road when he briefly glanced a couple of people struggling with a heavy piece of furniture. Lee dismissed them and kept on going until he looked in the rearview mirror and saw what the furniture had been blocking. He braked so fast that his truck fishtailed, almost ending up in the ditch.

Theirs could have been a remarkable and extremely satisfying love affair if only she hadn't been recently widowed. Lee could relate to that.

He chided himself for moving a little too fast with Allison, and while he stood looking in the mirror, he banged his hand on his head.

He sure hadn't felt like grieving for long after his wife died, and he patted himself on the back for putting on a good show at her funeral. He cried and carried on, all the while he was doing a little happy dance on the inside. It was liberating. No more being constrained by the binding elements of marriage, though he did live up to the part about 'until death do us part'. And that honey-do list was something he never missed.

At the funeral he had taken a little look-see on who all had attended, especially the ladies, ranking them on a scale of one to ten on merits like bust size, clothing, posture, hair length. Things like that were important to Lee.

A wedding band had never stopped Lee from pursuing his goal of getting as many ladies in bed as often as he could. The pickins' were getting mighty slim these days and Lee had hoped the big funeral announcement would draw some new blood. He was disappointed because the only new blood he was interested in was Allison Hartley.

Lee had been very patient with Allison, and he checked off all her merits like a grade school teacher grading a scoring sheet. Allison scored an "A" in Lee's book, mostly, except for a B minus up top, but he could overlook that shortcoming.

Unbeknownst to most people, Lee had taken out a million dollar policy on his wife. My, oh my, hadn't that come in handy? A couple of years before his wife died, he started noticing things about her that were out of the ordinary. She had developed a hoarse cough, shortness of breath, started wheezing, and had dropped a few pounds without even trying. Being the astute man Lee was, he knew something was wrong when she didn't even have the energy to do her favorite things, not to mention the lack of activity in their marital bed.

Unwilling to alert his doctor to his wife's symptoms, which he assured her was from working too hard, Lee went to the local library and Googled her symptoms. It was a grocery list of what she was suffering from. He convinced her to agree to a million dollar policy. With her holding down an eight to five job with health insurance and a 401K while Lee worked the ranch, if something happened to her, their kids wouldn't have an inheritance. It had worked like a charm.

A couple of years later, she was pushing up daisies. Literally, because Lee had planted some Gerber daisies on her grave. Wasn't that a nice touch? He thought so.

Now though, Lee was getting mighty lonely, not to mention his manly needs going unfulfilled. He kept up the facade of a brokenhearted husband for a few months, and couldn't for the life of him understand why Allison couldn't do the same.

He had been very patient.

An effing year of being patient!

Allison had held him off long enough, telling him she was still grieving over her dead husband and couldn't imagine dating anyone for a very long time, explaining it wouldn't be fair to his memory. What was the guy's name? Dale, Delbert? Lee couldn't recall, thinking it was some sissy-ass name not worthy of him remembering. And every time Allison mentioned her husband's name, Lee flipped off the listening switch in his brain.

And what was with her talking about him all the time? Every time they got together she started talking about him and how they first met, how they fell in love, what he liked to do, how good he was at fixing things, how there wasn't anything he wouldn't do for her. The guy was practically a saint, and Lee was starting to feel mighty inadequate next to that dead guy. The guy deserved a punch, but he was dead, and you can't beat up a dead guy.

Lee liked things in order too, and so did Allison by the looks of her housekeeping skills. Her neatness would come in handy when they got married because he wouldn't tolerate a messy house.

When Lee's sons moved out of the house and went to college the first thing he did was to get rid of their bedrooms, making them into his office and workout rooms, over the protests of his wife. He didn't care that his kids didn't like it either. The less they came around the better, and since their mom had died they hadn't made one trip to see their old man. Now wasn't that selfish?

And that dog of his wife's? Some useless little yapping white fluffy dog his wife had named Butterball. Lee couldn't stand the sight of the prissy dog. He kept the dog for a while after his wife died, but after numerous times of the dog messing on the carpet, Lee had had enough. One night he stuffed the dog in a bag, threw her in the car and drove far away, down the interstate until he came to a rest stop. He picked up the cowering dog from the back seat, and when he was sure nobody was around, he ran to the back of the rest stop and got rid of her.

Good riddance.

She was probably coyote bait by now.

His thoughts turned back to Allison. If Allison's kid was twelve that meant Lee only had to put up with him for five more years until Lee shipped him off to out-of-state college then he could have Allison all to himself. Five years wasn't too much of a sacrifice because she'd still be young, they'd have the whole house, the two of them alone and Lee could imagine plenty of ways she could entertain him. Plus she could serve him breakfast in bed. Yeah, Lee could hold out until then.

Time to step up to the plate.

He checked the time. Seven-thirty a.m. Sunday morning. In thirty minutes Allison should be sitting out on her front porch with a cup of coffee like she always did on Sunday mornings. Lee could concoct some reason to drive by her house. The excuse of getting a Sunday paper always worked well and he hadn't used that too many times, so she shouldn't be suspicious of him yet.

He threw on a pair of jeans, a clean shirt, work boots, put on his hat, and he was out the door.

He also had the idea to stop by Crystal Moore's place. He needed a little female company of the carnal kind, and since Crystal didn't run at the mouth like most of the women he knew, well, Sunday morning was shaping up fine and dandy.

Chapter 12

Sunday was a day Allison could relax. She did not get the storm she wished for, only more of the same dry heat and blistering high temperatures. Her shop stayed open six days a week, and even though most of the tourist shops stayed open on Sunday, she really needed to rest and spend time with Josh.

When Allison first moved to Bastrop, she had rented a cozy two bedroom house five miles west of town on an unpaved farm-to-market road with houses intermittently spaced on either side, situated on tracts of land anywhere from one to thirty acres.

She'd picked that place because of the reasonable rent and the fact that the landlord really wanted someone to occupy the house before he put it up for sale.

Allison and the landlord had a deal: if Allison cleaned up the place, did inside painting, and basically spruced up the place and made it have more curb appeal, he promised to knock off one hundred dollars of rent every month. The clincher that sealed the deal: he gave her first right of refusal on the sale.

Early on, when she had first moved in, she cleaned the hardwood floors and put wood-colored putty in the cracks or holes. She painted the walls a muted beige color and scrubbed the stains off of the linoleum floors. For the stubborn stains or nicks, she used white-out to fill in the black gouges. Not the best repair, yet it worked, and unless someone scrutinized it on their hands and knees, it was unnoticeable.

In her downtime at the shop, she made coverings for pillows, reupholstered chairs, and made curtains until the cottage looked like it could be on the cover of one of those home and garden magazines displayed in bookstores, all bright and pretty with a full spectrum of summer colors.

In the detached garage with a dirt floor and cobwebs strung all over the place, Allison found a plethora of rusty garden tools and broken pots. She super-glued the broken pottery pieces together to use as planters for red geraniums. She filled the planters with enriched soil she bought at the local nursery then placed the planters full of geraniums on the slatted front porch.

Over the next year, Josh had made friends, was doing well in school, making the honor roll every six weeks, and was becoming a leader in his team sports. Josh liked the place and the extra acreage that came along with the house. He and his friends spent many hours in the woods and pines behind the house playing in the ramshackle fort they had built, or exploring the endless trails. That and the fact that her shop had finally become profitable made three excellent reasons to offer to buy the place.

After the year was up, the landlord decided to sell the place, and as he promised he gave Allison the first right of refusal. Taking out a mortgage was a little scary, yet she had saved money for a down payment, and managed to get a reasonable interest rate.

Owning her first home was liberating and she took great pride in it.

In the year Allison had occupied the cottage she had really made the place look splendid, especially since the previous tenant hadn't taken care of it. When she moved in, scuff marks were all over the wood floors, the bathroom tile had years of ground-in dirt and grime, and there wasn't a single curtain in the whole house. Not to mention an impervious layer of dust that caked the house from baseboard to ceiling that was so thick it took a spatula to scrape it off.

The whole house consisted of a working kitchen overlooking the den, two bedrooms down the hall, and a bathroom she shared with Josh. It was enough room, affording them a modicum of privacy so the two of them wouldn't trip over one another.

So far, so good.

Holding a cup of coffee, she opened the screen door and stepped out onto the porch, taking in the brief coolness of the early morning that had not yet given way to the oppressive heat of the day. Birdsong melody filled the air and Allison took a moment to listen to nature's music.

Drought resistant roadside flowers lined the county road, draping it in swaths of red and orange Indian blankets, burgundy wine cups, and her favorite pink evening primroses. A little ways down the road, a seasonal creek ran across the dip in the road where minnows hid in deep puddles in the shade of overhanging branches.

She took a seat on the wooden rocking chair she had bought earlier in the summer at a garage sale. When she sat down, it creaked under her weight.

Swirling curls of steam rose off the coffee, and Allison sipped carefully.

Bluebonnets had gone to seed, replaced by hotter weather and drought resistant flowers, yet even those were droopy from lack of rain. Indian paintbrushes amidst black-eyed Susans and sunflowers had taken residence on both sides of the gravelly driveway leading to her cottage.

Somewhere a cicada chirped, a bee buzzed, and a cardinal sang. Clouds floated in the sky and a hawk perched on a treetop, scanning the nearby fields for a hapless field mouse or a fox squirrel.

The morning would have been absolutely perfect if Doug had been with her, and as she rocked back and forth she imagined they would have lounged the morning away on the porch, the sun rising over the treetops, talking about the future. She wondered why they had stayed in the city instead of living their dream in a quiet place like she had now. She thought it strange how Doug had to die in order for her to find peace.

When it was quiet and still, Allison thought often of Doug and Madison, their memories filling the empty space in her heart.

Doug wasn't here, and never would be, and neither would Maddy. Her chest tightened and she shook her head, trying to dismiss the melancholy thoughts. It would be better to focus on the here and now, instead of wondering about the 'what ifs'. Allison prided herself on being strong.

She had to be.

She had no other choice.

Her thoughts went to the conversation she had with Susan when she said she wasn't looking for a man. *"I know, Allie, but that's when you'll find one,"* Susan had said. Allison certainly wasn't looking for a husband, and even if on some level of consciousness she was, her antenna never buzzed, except for yesterday when her new customer walked into the store.

The reaction she had when they shook hands surprised her. His hands were warm and strong, yet not so much the bone-crunching as so many men were apt to do when shaking hands with a woman. Rather his handshake evoked reflections of 'this is who I am, this is me'. A slight smile crept across her face when she thought about him nearly flattening Susan when he walked into her store.

He? Shouldn't she say his name?

"Brendon." She said his name aloud, trying it out. She thought it had a nice ring to it.

The available bachelors in Bastrop were about as plenty as the rainfall in a desert Allison mused. Everyone was either married, too old, too young, too weird, or too something, and Allison had no interest in anyone she knew. She regretted dating Lee Mercer, and now he was becoming troublesome.

Her and Lee get together? Not in a thousand years.

She sipped again on her coffee.

When she saw him at the county fair, she would have to tell him in no uncertain language that their relationship was only casual, and they'd never be a couple. Hopefully, he'd get the message. If he didn't she wasn't sure what she would do.

Lee had told her about the history of the land she owned, at one time part of a 5,000 acre McMahon homestead of the 1800s.

He said the McMahon family heirs had to split the sprawling ranch, yet what remained could still be construed huge by today's standards. Five hundred acres of prime ranchland, crops, and timber was left of the once sprawling ranch. Local gossip said that the last remaining heir in the family had moved away years ago after some sort of tragedy. She had asked Lee about it. He'd said it had happened a long time ago, so no need to dredge up the past. It made her sad to think about how the once stately McMahon ranch house located about a mile past her place and down the road had fallen into disrepair.

Most of the house looked livable, while part of the house still had fingerprints of a fire with charred beams and boarded up windows.

The other day, she swore a light was on at the house, and every so often she had seen someone coming and going. She'd thought it might have been a real estate salesman. Dismissing the thought she took another sip of coffee.

"Wait a moment," Allison said out loud. She set her coffee cup down, got up from the rocker, and hurried back into the house. Where was the receipt her new customer gave her? Rummaging through yesterday's receipts which she kept in her briefcase, she found it. She read the name and gasped. *Brendon McMahon.* Now it made sense. *He* was the last remaining McMahon. How about that? Her new customer was an ancestor of one of the first homesteaders to the region.

Interesting.

She stuffed the receipt back into her briefcase and headed back to the porch where she retrieved her coffee. She leaned against one of the columns she had sanded and painted, satisfied at her handiwork and heeding the advice of her father that a thick layer of white paint did wonders for any old thing.

She had scoured flea markets and estate sales looking for old or chipped furniture that only needed a good cleaning or a new coat of paint. Sometimes when business was slow she'd close early and make a quick trip to Austin where she could hunt for bargains in the fabric stores, inspecting the remnant table for discontinued fabrics that would make good curtains. Several times Susan had encouraged her to start a web-based business of her handmade wares. "People like country things," Susan would always tell her, "especially people from the big cities, because country living has a certain allure. It's something they dream about. If you can bring a little bit of the country to the city, then do it." Allison was beginning to entertain that idea as a way to supplement her main means of supporting herself and

Josh.

Except she had her hands full at the moment and that idea would be for another time.

She stepped off the porch and walked down the steps leading to the gravel walkway. From there, she strolled a few steps to the road to pick a bouquet of wildflowers. She knew she wasn't supposed to, because it was actually illegal to pick roadside flowers. If the flowers weren't made to be so beautiful, she would not have picked them. Besides, only a grouch of a police officer would write a ticket for picking flowers.

The sound of a truck caught Allison's attention. The truck came closer then veered sharply, coming to a complete stop on the side of the road. Squinting through the streams of sunlight, Allison's shoulders drooped and her smile disappeared when she recognized the driver.

"Morning, Allison," Lee said, tipping his hat in cowboy fashion, his arm casually resting on the driver's side window.

Allison walked over to his truck, idling at an angle on the side of the road.

"Morning, Lee," she said. Her voice was devoid of inflection. She stepped back onto the driveway, careful not to mash down any of the flowers.

"Beautiful day we're having," Lee said.

Allison nodded.

"Say, I'm headed into town to get a Sunday newspaper. Do you need anything while I'm there?"

"No, thank you."

"Ice, groceries, anything?"

"Nope."

"Okay, I thought I'd be neighborly and ask." Lee put the truck in gear.

"Lee, wait a minute. Your pants are ready. I had to bring them home for some hand-stitching," Allison said.

"I can pick them up on Monday," Lee offered.

She was halfway up the porch when she called back, "No need to now." She ran inside, retrieved the pants, and returned to the truck. "Here you go," she said handing the pants to Lee.

"Thank you very much," Lee said. He placed them on the seat. "I'm looking forward to seeing you at the county fair."

"Right," Allison said flatly. "I'd better get going. I need to fix Josh some breakfast."

He drove off and rounded the corner, out of sight. Four more weeks and she'd be rid of Lee. Allison felt better already and that slump in her shoulders magically disappeared and the spring in her step was back.

She headed back to the cottage, lazily kicking pebbles in front of her, watching them skittle across the road. She skipped up the steps of her cottage, studied the geraniums, and decided to twist off a couple of stalks so that she could add them to the roadside flowers for a bouquet.

Flowers always reminded her of Maddy, and as she held the gold locket she thought about her daughter and how much she missed her. Maddy loved flowers and all things girly. She would have been six by now, preparing to enter first grade.

Allison smiled at her memory of Maddy 'washing' dishes, standing on a stepstool at the kitchen sink, splashing and making a mess with the soapy suds. Memories of her daughter comforted Allison, and only recently could she think of her without crying.

She gathered the geranium stalks and went inside, careful not to let the screen door slam behind her. She never liked it when Josh ran into the house flinging the screen door open so hard that when it slammed shut, it rattled the windows.

She found a vase, filled it halfway with water, and

placed the flowers on the kitchen table. She mixed up a batch of pancake mix and got out a cast iron skillet she'd bought at a garage sale. With some curing, it was good as new. Add a little bit of oil to the bottom, swirl it around, heat the skillet to the perfect temperature and the pancakes would beat any ten dollar roadhouse pancake.

Josh walked into the kitchen and sat down at the table, rubbing his eyes.

"Hey, sleepyhead, want some breakfast?" Allison asked. She popped four slices of bacon into the microwave.

Josh nodded. "Can I have two pancakes with chocolate chips?"

Normally Allison wouldn't allow Josh to have chocolate in the morning. Since it was Sunday, and since he had done all his chores on Saturday, it couldn't hurt. "Sure, why not? I'll sprinkle some in for you. Want it in a shape of a happy face?"

"Mom! I'm not a baby anymore. I'm almost thirteen."

"Your dad always liked it when I made him smiley face pancakes."

"I'm not Dad."

That statement stung at Allison, causing her heart to skip a beat. Her little boy was growing up right before her eyes, and that sweet little boy who wanted to cuddle with her only a few years ago was slowly fading away. Looking at him now, it appeared he had sprouted an inch overnight, and his voice sounded a little deeper. Maybe that's why he was so grumpy; he was having growing pains.

"You look like your dad did when he was your age," Allison said. She motioned to the fireplace mantel. "Like in the picture where he is standing next to his dad."

Josh looked in the direction of the fireplace. "I miss Dad."

Allison put down the spatula she was holding, gazed at him lovingly, wishing she could hug away Josh's pain. Maybe that's what he needed. She went to Josh, stood next to him, and put her hands out indicating a hug.

"No, Mom. I'm not a baby."

"You're still my son," she said, holding out her arms. "I miss him too."

"I know."

"Hug?"

"I guess so, but don't hug me anymore in front of my friends."

"Okay, promise." Allison gave him a hug and went back to the stove to check on the pancakes.

Josh hung his head. "I can't even remember what Dad's voice sounds like. Sometimes I dream about him. We're playing baseball like we used to and when I wake up I think for just a moment that he's still here." Josh picked up a fork, twirling it in his hand. "I'm the only kid at school who doesn't have a dad."

"You do have a dad. One who loved you very much."

"You know what I mean." Josh put the fork down and made direct eye contact with his mother. "Why did Dad have to die?"

"I don't know." Allison turned away from her son, afraid he might notice her deception. She reached for a towel and folded it then stashed it in the corner of the counter. Without much conviction she said, "It was his time. He had a heart attack." She paused before adding flatly, "Heart problems run in his family."

Josh was silent for a moment. "Go ahead and put the chocolates in a shape of smiley face."

Allison poured Josh a glass of milk, waited for the chocolate to melt, then served him two large pancakes with butter and syrup, along with four pieces of bacon. Josh scarfed everything down then asked for another pancake.

"We have enough batter to make another one," Allison said.

"Mom, have you eaten?" Josh asked.

"I had a bowl of oatmeal and coffee."

"Gross," Josh said, making a face. "I *hate* oatmeal. And why would anybody drink coffee?"

Allison laughed. "It's not so bad. When you get older you can't eat the things you used to when you were younger. Your palate changes and–"

"What's a palate?"

"It's the way things taste to you."

"Oh," Josh grunted. "It changes when you're older, like when you're twenty?"

Allison laughed. "That's not old."

"Then what does that make you?"

"Joshua Douglas Hartley! I can't believe you said that."

"What did I say?" Josh asked. His eyes were about as big as his open mouth.

"Never mind. Finish your breakfast."

Josh finished his last pancake and took his dishes to the sink. "Hey, Mom?"

"Yes?"

"Can you throw me some balls this morning? I need the practice."

"You know I'm not very good at that."

"That's the point," Josh said.

Allison looked at him quizzically.

"It keeps me on my toes."

"Oh, I get it," she said, laughing. "You go change and after I clean up the kitchen we'll play."

After Josh ran off, Allison walked over to the kitchen table, leaned over, drew in a deep breath of the roadside flowers. She sneezed. Sponge in hand, she wiped down the table and straightened the tablecloth. It only took a minute to clean things up, and doing things when they needed to be done was better than letting everything pile up for a marathon session of cleaning.

Back at the sink, she plugged the stopper and filled the sink, squeezing in a few drops of blue dishwashing soap into the running water. One thing she did miss was the dishwasher at her old apartment. However, the view here at her cottage more than made up for having to hand wash dishes.

Maddy definitely would have liked this place.

Allison missed the companionship of her husband, little everyday things that a wife and husband talk to each other about, like how the day had gone, or what to prepare for dinner, people they talked to during the day, finishing each other's sentences, and laughing about it afterwards. Little things like that. Always someone waiting to hear your footsteps at the end of the day.

She especially missed the times they would lay on the sofa together, sipping wine and watching a late night movie.

The conversation was different when Allison talked to Josh, mainly focusing on his life and what he liked to do. Baseball was always a topic of conversation, yet she didn't know the first thing about baseball, other than first, second, and third bases. She knew what a homerun meant, what a walk meant, foul balls, how many innings made up a game, and now that she mentally checked off what she knew, her knowledge wasn't *that* bad, even though Josh teased her mercilessly about the game.

She had come a long way from the day when Doug and Madison had died, successfully burying the rage over the death of Doug. She hadn't realized he had been so desperate that robbing a store seemed the only option. Why didn't she pick up on the clues? She supposed it was because she had focused all her energy on Madison. It didn't leave much left over for Doug. As a wife, she had failed him. If only he had confided in her, they could have made it together, instead he had acted alone and it had cost him his life.

It was history now and she needed to concentrate on building her business, and making sure Josh had a stable home environment.

It was time to move on, although where to, she wasn't sure.

After Allison finished washing dishes, she stacked them in the dish rack to dry.

"Mom, I'm ready," Josh said as he came out of his bedroom. He was palming a baseball and thumping it against his gloved hand.

"Ten more minutes and I promise. I still have a little more cleaning to do."

"Mom!" Josh pleaded. "I'm putting the timer on for exactly ten minutes then I'm making you come out with me."

It was during times like this when Allison really missed Doug, when Josh really needed a father. And to think the teenage years were just starting.

What was she going to do?

Chapter 13

After a restless night, Brendon woke up early on Sunday morning and decided to pay a visit to the cemetery where his parents and sister were buried. It was a local country cemetery not far from where Brendon lived. Gravestones dated all the way back to the 1800s. Many of the names etched on the old tombstones were McMahon, great-grandparents, distant relatives. For such a large and successful family, Brendon was the only male heir.

Their graves were side by side and marked with a flat placard with their names, birth, and death dates etched into it. He couldn't afford one of those big marble headstones, and besides, who was he trying to impress? In a hundred years, it wouldn't matter. For that matter, even one year. When a person died, a lot died with them, but life went on and Brendon still had a lot of life to live, even if it was by himself.

He placed a bouquet of roadside flowers at the graves of his family and said a silent prayer before walking back to his truck. He started the engine, looped the truck around, and headed to the house he now owned and was renovating.

He rolled his truck to a stop in front of the old house and killed the ignition. He swung the door open and was stepping out when a loose piece of metal on the side of the truck caught his pants, tearing them around the pocket.

"Great," he muttered. He contemplated whether or not to throw the pants away. He didn't have the slightest clue how to repair them. He was thinking maybe some superglue and some duct tape might do the trick when another idea popped into his head.

This would give him a perfect excuse to see Allison again. He could drop by her store this morning to see her. Surely her store was open on Sunday, everything else was.

Allison.

He was already calling her by her first name, like he knew her. She occupied his thoughts during the day and night, and even when he didn't think he was thinking of her, he was. While he drove along the roads or did work around his ranch, he had imaginary conversations with her, little unimportant things, things people talk about when getting to know each other. Sometimes he rehearsed how he would tell her about the circumstances around Doug's death, how sorry he was, how he wished he could take Doug's place. It drove him crazy, going over and over it in his mind, even waking him up in the middle of the night where he would lay in bed, his hands clasped behind his head.

How would he tell her? He would have to pick the right time and place, and like Krishna had said, when the time was right the words would come to him.

Now, though, he was looking at the tear in his pants. He needed to make his pants last a little longer because there wasn't much leeway for new clothes in his meager budget. Buying the wrong length of pants so he could have an excuse to meet Allison was an impulsive purchase, constricting his monthly budget even more. Come to think of it, she hadn't even measured him. Maybe her tailoring skills were to the point she didn't have to measure. Brendon didn't mind, it would give him yet another chance to see her.

He thought about the budget for home repairs, thinking the money would last about a year, possibly a little longer, then after that he planned to go into nearby Austin and look for a job.

He slammed the truck door shut and the commotion roused the attention of Bo. He was becoming one hundred percent country hound dog, and although he wouldn't win any purebred competition or beauty contests, he was the perfect dog. He was alert, clear eyed, had hearing that could detect a mouse twenty yards away, and Brendon was quite happy to have the companionship the dog offered.

All fifty pounds of affable hound dog came sauntering off the porch, tongue hanging out, slobber sloshing, and tail thumping. When Bo went to jump on Brendon, he stepped to the side, motioning for Bo not to jump.

"Dang it, Bo," Brendon said playfully. "You need to learn some manners. No jumping because I can't get my pants dirty. I need to take them to Allison to get them repaired. Understand?"

Bo thumped his tail and wiggled from side to side.

"Good." Brendon patted Bo on the head.

Standing in the front yard with Bo beside him, Brendon took a quick scan of the two-story house built in the early 1900s. The frame and foundation were still solid, though he would have to replace the rotting columns supporting the front porch roof. There were four of them, and at first Brendon thought he could simply paint them, and he had tried doing that until he noticed at times he was painting about five layers of paint, and not actual wood. What looked like wood was actually layers upon layers of paint. It was a wonder the whole porch hadn't caved in. He'd have to work on that right away.

The planks looked to be in good shape. He'd have to sand most of them, and perhaps he could save some time and rent a heavy duty sander instead of trying to do it by hand.

The roof would have to be replaced, and the part of the house damaged by fire would have to be completely stripped to the studs. Even after two decades of elapsed time, his emotions were still raw, and he had a difficult time even walking into that part of the house. He'd leave the remodeling of that part of the house for later. From the road, it didn't look too bad since most of the damage was in the back. The rooms had been boarded up from the main part of the house long ago, so unless he tore down the boards, he could leave it as it was.

If he tackled one job at a time, he'd get it done over the course of a year or two.

Brendon walked up the creaky stairs, Bo a step behind him. He opened the screen door and said, "Come on, Bo. I've got to change into another pair of pants."

The dog expertly slid between Brendon and the door frame, went over to his water bowl in the kitchen, slopped water, then dribbled it back to his favorite corner by the fireplace where Brendon had put down a piece of carpet for Bo to sleep on.

Bo was scratching a flea when a sound caught his attention. Pricking his ears, he let out a hound-dog bellow. Brendon turned and glanced through the windows to see a truck coming to a stop at his gravel driveway.

"Come on, Bo, let's go see who it is."

"Howdy, neighbor," a man called, getting out of his truck.

"Hello," Brendon replied, shading his eyes from the morning sun-glint. He took a few steps off of the porch to meet who he surmised was a neighbor. A flicker of recognition captured Brendon when he realized it was the same jerk that had been in Allison's shop.

Bo lifted his muzzle, tasting the air.

Sniff, sniff.

He growled low and throaty, recognizing the scent of the man from the rest stop. He was the one who had thrown away the little white dog. Bo wasn't the weak, pitiful animal he had been. He was strong now, confident, and unafraid.

"Bo! What's wrong with you? Stop it! Understand!"

Bo looked at Brendon then back at the man, staring dog daggers at him.

"Sit!" When Bo didn't react, Brendon tapped his behind. "Sit."

Bo reluctantly sat.

"Sorry about that. I'm not sure what's gotten into him."

"No problem. I'm Lee Mercer."

"Brendon McMahon." He reluctantly extended a hand to shake.

"McMahon, you said?"

"That's right."

"Hmm, oh wait. You must be Jeff's son."

"I am. Did you know my dad?" Brendon asked with all the enthusiasm of a kid sitting in the dentist's office waiting for a root canal.

"Not really," Lee said. "My wife and I bought our place up the road a few months before the fire. I only spoke to your dad a few times. It was a terrible tragedy, you being so young, and not being able to–"

"It was a long time ago," Brendon interrupted.

"I see. Are your parents still living?"

"No."

"Sorry to hear that." Lee looked around and scuffed the ground with the toe of his boot. "My wife's buried in the cemetery." He jerked his head to the north. "She's been gone a while."

"I'm sorry to hear that. My parents are buried there too."

"Sister?"

"Yes," Brendon replied.

Lee thought that over. Something in the way Brendon said 'yes' caught Lee off guard and made him wonder why Brendon was being curt. The expression on his face was one of disdain, and Lee should know about that look because he was a master at it. Maybe it was his imagination, or maybe McMahon was tired or had broken up with a girlfriend. Whatever. It didn't give him carte blanche to be rude. It was impossible they had met before because Lee didn't recall ever meeting him. Still, his curiosity got the best of him.

"Have we met?" he asked.

"Don't think so."

"Hmm." The verbal pause gave Lee time to look at Bo. "Nice dog you got there. I used to have a little dog." Lee scratched the side of his head and glanced away. "Actually my wife's dog. The cutest sweetest little thing, named Butterball. She went downhill fast after my wife died. Nothing the vet could do would help. I had to put her to sleep."

Brendon noticed the body language immediately recognizing Lee was lying. No telling what he had done to that poor dog.

Lee bent over to pet Bo on the head and without warning Bo lashed out and snapped at Lee's hand, drawing blood.

With lightning fast speed, Lee withdrew his hand and glowered at the dog.

Bo stood his ground and glared at the man he remembered smelling of booze and sweat. Bo swung his head from side to side taking in more of his smell. This was definitely the man who had dumped the little fluffy white dog, the dog Bo had comforted, had helped, and shared his home with. The dog who'd disappeared.

Bow growled low in his throat, deep and guttural.

"Take it easy, Bo," Brendon commanded.

Bo didn't hear the words, instead his eyes were lasers on Lee. This man was bad.

"Bo!" Brendon yelled.

Bo took a step back and sat on his haunches, looking to Brendon for guidance. Brendon made eye contact with Bo, and made a slight motion with his hand.

"Look what your dog did! What the hell is wrong with it! All I was trying to do was to pet it." He thrust out his hand. "Look at that. I'm bleeding. Aren't you going to do anything?"

"Bo's a good judge of character and I don't think he likes you."

"Who gives a crap if your dog likes me. He bit me!"

"Anyone knows not to try to pet a strange dog on the top of their head. You didn't ask either."

"Huh?" Lee was incredulous. "I need *permission* to pet a dog?"

"That's right. If you would have asked me I would have said no because Bo doesn't like strangers petting him."

"Is that so?"

"Uh huh."

"That no good mangy dog needs to be taught a lesson!" Lee exclaimed. He took a step forward, readying his boot to kick Bo.

In an instant, Bo's easygoing personality changed, and for a large dog he sprung up on all fours with the graceful agility of a cat. His muscles rippled, his teeth bared in a snarl ready to defend himself. Bo neither growled nor barked, remaining perfectly rigid without breaking eye contact with the angry man.

The dog's sudden transformation startled Lee and he instinctively stepped back. He reached for his clip-it knife he kept in his pocket, and with a gesture he had done a thousand times before, he flipped it open.

Brendon thought and acted quickly, searching for anything he might use as a weapon. In an instant, he grabbed a piece of lumber he found over to the side of the road and turned back to face Lee, slapping the board against the palm of his left hand.

The sound caught Lee's attention.

"Don't even think about hurting my dog," Brendon said.

Lee thought that last sentence over while he sized up his new neighbor. About six feet tall, lanky, well-muscled, and he had an edge about him that made Lee leery. Maybe the guy had some military training or something with the way he was acting so authoritative. He was a little too cool, and it had been a long time since anyone had challenged Lee. The way he held the board was disconcerting too, like he wasn't bluffing, like he would actually use it. Something about the way the guy held himself snapped Lee out of his trance.

"You'd better put a muzzle on that dog before he bites somebody else," he spat.

"He didn't bite you. He warned you. If Bo bit you, you'd know it."

"If you're not going to do something about that dog, I will!" Lee palmed his knife and faced the dog.

Brendon didn't change his expression. "I wouldn't do that if I was you."

A silent moment went by, then another. Both men stood still, measuring each other.

Bo panted in the hot sun.

The droning of a low flying airplane broke the silence.

Lee Mercer had never met this man before, and at first glance, the man could have been any city dweller trying to escape the big city. Those guys were soft, unaccustomed to the manual work needed to ranch. A

93

day's work usually exhausted those kinds, but this guy? There was something too casual in the way he stood and the way he handled himself. Everybody in these parts knew Lee and knew to kowtow to him.

"I remember you now. Last time I saw you, you were a snot nosed bratty kid."

"I'm not a kid anymore. Maybe you can bully kids and dogs, but if I was you, I'd get in my truck and leave."

The heat rose in Lee's face and that vein on the side of his head mirrored his rapidly beating heart. "Some thanks I get for trying to be neighborly."

Brendon slapped the two by four in his hand.

Lee knew when he had been beat. Admitting it to the man was another matter.

Lee snorted. "Your dog aint' worth it. And as far as you are concerned," he said pointing his index finger at Brendon, "we'll settle this another time."

Chapter 14

Brendon felt utter contempt toward Lee Mercer. While he had been on the police force, he had lots of dealings with those kinds of guys, a monster lurking behind a facade of geniality. Wife beaters and animal abusers came to mind, and any guy who raised a hand to a woman or beat a dog needed the strong arm of the law to bring them down a peg or two.

In a town as small as Bastrop, Brendon knew there would be more run-ins with Lee, and he'd have to be on his toes watching out for any ambushes the guy might have planned. First things first, he checked the time. It was almost 9 am, and by the time he made it into town, Allison's shop would probably be open.

Brendon looked at Bo. "I didn't like that guy one bit."

With confirming eyes and a cocked head, Bo understood the intonation.

Grabbing his torn pants and keys from the house, Brendon asked, "Wanna go for a ride and get outta here?"

Bo wagged his tail.

"I thought so. Come on. Let's go."

Brendon drove along the farm-to-market road, his left arm resting on the driver's side window, Bo next to him in the front seat, peering out the window, the warm air rippling his fur. No riding in the truck bed for Bo. One jostle or bump and Bo would be thrown out, lost or hurt, and in this heat and drought, he wouldn't last long. Brendon reached over to Bo and taking a handful of fur, massaged the dog's back, ran his hand along his haunches, and then up to his face.

A dense forest of pine trees blanketed the countryside, so thick sometimes the sun was obscured. There wasn't a cloud in the sky, or the slightest promise of one, only more of the unrelenting heat.

It was going to be another scorcher today.

The heat and drought worried Brendon.

Among the greenery were signs of dead or distressed pines with brown pine needles clinging to dead limbs. Entire patches of pine trees were dead. The pines had survived the eons, were there before written history, surviving the last ice age, human encroachment, wildfires, drought, logging, and insect infestations. Currently, they were struggling to outlast the biblical drought.

If they didn't get rain soon, one errant cigarette or campfire embers hit by a gust of wind would be catastrophic, and with only one road out of here, well, Brendon didn't want to revisit that scenario or a fire because if he thought about fires, he'd be reliving his childhood tragedy. His parents were adamant it wasn't his fault, telling him he was only a child, and shouldn't have been left at home. Brendon's parents blamed themselves, and it had destroyed them.

Brendon vowed not to let it destroy him.

He drove along the winding road, his thoughts taking him to Allison. He remembered how stunningly beautiful she was. A smile broke across his face at how tongue tied he must have appeared, how foolish he must have looked when he almost trampled her friend.

His eyes caught movement at the house to the left.

Jolted out of reminiscing, he slammed on the brakes.

Bo rolled off the front seat and onto the floorboard. The truck fishtailed, leaving a spray of flying gravel.

Maybe Brendon's eyes were playing tricks on him.

Maybe that wasn't Allison who was playing catch in the front yard with a boy who must have been her son.

Maybe she didn't live on the same country road as he did.

She was wearing blue jean shorts, white sneakers, and a cute little blousy top decorated in a flowery pattern. Her tousled sandy colored hair fell softly over her shoulders.

Allison and Josh stopped playing and turned in the direction of the truck. It was an older model Ford truck, mostly white except for the dents and scratches along the side. The truck backed up and pulled into the driveway.

"Who's that, Mom?" Josh asked.

"Beats me," Allison said, trying to see through the windshield that reflected the pine trees. She squinted against the morning sun-glare then recognized the driver as the customer who had come in on Saturday. How could she forget a man as handsome as Brendon McMahon?

Her cheeks became flushed with heat, and she fanned her face with the baseball glove.

Josh saw his mother's expression and rosy face. "You know him?" Josh asked in a hushed tone. Allison shushed him.

Brendon killed the engine, stepped out, and held the door open for Bo, who promptly loped to a tree to sit in the shade.

"Hello," Allison said.

"Hello," Brendon replied. Feeling quite sheepish, he tugged on his cap, scratched the side of his jeans. He told

Bo to stay. "I was heading into town to see if your store was open."

"On Sunday morning?" Allison asked.

"Aren't most stores open on Sunday? Blue laws aren't in effect anymore, are they?"

"Oh, no, those laws were abolished a long time ago except for liquor," Allison explained. "Mine's closed, though." Facing Josh, she tossed him a ball, or tried to, because Josh had to run up to catch the ball.

"Mom throws like a girl," Josh said, tossing the ball back to Allison.

"That's because I *am* a girl." Allison held out her gloved hand only to miss catching the ball and have it thump to the ground. "Bet I can sew better than both of you put together."

Josh rolled his eyes. "Like there's ever a *sew-off.*"

"It makes us a good living," Allison retorted without missing a beat. "Brendon, to answer your question, only some of the stores are open. It's mostly restaurants that open up around noon in time for the Sunday church crowd." Allison pitched the ball back to Josh. He caught it then threw a grounder to her. She bent over to get it, only to miss it. The ball whizzed by her and bounced into the grass.

"I'll get that," Brendon said, running after the ball.

"Did you need something at my shop?" Allison asked. "And before I forget to tell you, you ran out of the store before I had a chance to measure you."

"Oh, I thought maybe you were so good you didn't need to take measurements."

"I'm good, just not that good." Allison paused. "Come by my store on Monday and we'll get you fixed up." She twirled a lock of hair. "What did you need today, exactly?"

"I tore my jeans on a piece of metal sticking out of my truck. I was hoping you could repair them," Brendon

98

said. He tossed the arcing ball to Josh. It made a solid thud when Josh caught it.

"Bring those in on Monday too," Allison said.

"Good throw," Josh said, looking at Brendon. "I'm Josh."

"Nice to meet you. I'm Brendon McMahon."

Josh nodded. "You play baseball?"

"Not since I was in high school."

"What position did you play?"

"Shortstop," Brendon said.

Josh thought about that as he jostled the ball back and forth into his glove. He eyed Bo. "What's your dog's name?"

"Bo."

"We don't have a dog. Mom won't let me get one." When he noticed his mom looking away, Josh tossed another fast grounder to her. It skidded into the flowers.

"Josh! Are you doing that on purpose?" Allison asked, running after the ball.

"No. You know you aren't very good at playing baseball."

"Here, let me," Brendon said. "I'll toss him some balls."

"Thanks" Allison said. She handed her glove to Brendon.

Brendon slipped his hand into the glove, and it was like it had been custom made for him. "It fits like a glove." He waited for a response. "No pun intended."

"Lame," Josh said, rolling his eyes.

"Josh!" Allison scolded.

"What!" He shot his mom a teenager-worthy death stare. "It *was* a lame joke."

"Whose glove is this?" Brendon asked. "It can't be yours, Josh. It's too big."

"It belonged to Josh's dad, Doug." Allison recognized the look on Brendon's face as an expression of knowledge or sympathy. She wondered if she had mentioned Doug was deceased when she and Brendon met for first time. It wasn't a topic she randomly spoke about, especially to a stranger.

"He's deceased," she said.

Brendon wasn't quite sure what to say and the normal *I'm sorry* wouldn't suffice. How could he ever tell her *how* sorry he was? What would she do if she knew she was talking to the man who had killed her husband, even though the shooting had been justified and Brendon had been cleared of any wrongdoing?

"I'm sorry," he said. The glove felt constricting. "Here, maybe I shouldn't use it, being your husband's and all." He took off the glove and offered it back to Allison.

"Oh no, please use it."

"I'm really sorry about your husband," Brendon said. He looked down at the ground and kicked the toe of his shoe in the dirt. "Really sorry."

Allison mulled over his answer, considering why he was so sorry. "Did you know my husband?"

Brendon looked up. "No." It was the truth; he hadn't known the man, so technically he wasn't lying. "If there is anything I can do, let me know. Really, I'm serious."

"I may take you up on that someday."

"Mom, it's getting hot, can you make some lemonade, please?"

"Sure," Allison answered.

"Be sure to put lots of sugar in it!" Josh yelled. "None of that fake pink stuff. That tastes gross, just like coffee does!"

"Five cups of sugar and one lemon coming up," Allison said, cracking a smile.

Brendon waited until Allison had gone inside before he said, "Does your mom really put in five cups of sugar?"

Josh shrugged. "Probably."

Standing at the kitchen sink, Allison placed a cutting board on the counter, dug around searching for the lemon squeezer, then retrieved a bowl of lemons from the refrigerator. From the moment she had seen Brendon in her store she had been immediately attracted to him, a fact hard for her to admit. Ever since Doug had died, she had busied herself to the point she didn't have time to think about dating anyone. Now that Brendon was so close, her thoughts wandered to him.

What did she know about him? He obviously had manners, and had an immediate rapport with both herself and Josh, and a sense of humor didn't hurt either. He treated his dog in a kind manner, and had genuinely apologized to Susan when he almost knocked her down. Allison smiled. Such minute details to try to form a complete picture of someone, yet they were enough for Allison because she noticed such things.

Methodically, she washed the lemons thoroughly before cutting them in half. Next, she hand-squeezed them. After she had squeezed the last drops out, she tossed the rinds in the garbage.

What was he doing here? Was he seeing anyone?

She retrieved a pitcher from the cabinet, poured the lemon juice in, added cold water and sugar, stirring it until all the sugar had dissolved. She tasted it, thinking, *perfect*. One more little dash of sugar and she'd have the perfect blend of tangy tartness and sugary sweetness. She added a tray of ice-cubes and voila! Delicious homemade lemonade that would beat any store-bought mixture.

She tried to reassure herself that Brendon was only a customer, nothing more, and what man didn't buy pants too long, and since she was one of only two tailors in town, it made good enough sense that he found her store.

Brendon's attitude and the way he carried himself

spoke of a self-assured man, an honest man, one who reminded her of Doug, one who could take care of a family and a wife. She longingly gazed out the window upon Josh and Brendon playing catch. It could have been Doug and Josh, but she shook off the comparison.

It was coming up on late-morning and the sun fully shone above the tops of the pines. The sky was hot and clear, the air heavy and thick covering the land like a heated blanket. Birds flitted in the dry tangle of underbrush in the field behind her home, and grasshoppers and cicadas filled the air with steady chirps.

Nearly twenty minutes had gone by and as Allison was pouring three glasses of lemonade, Josh and Brendon ran in, out of breath, sweat mopping their hair and faces. She caught a whiff of manly sweatiness. It wasn't unpleasant, only something Allison noticed. For a brief moment she thought about Doug coming home after working all day doing manual labor, making cabinets. He always smelled of fresh wood.

"Mom?"

"Hmm?"

"You okay? You look like you're a million miles away."

"I'm fine." Allison scratched the side of her head. "Fine, really, I am."

"Can Bo come inside? Please? It's so hot outside, and he's panting and looks really hot."

"I guess it's alright," Allison said.

By the time Allison finished her sentence Josh had run over to the front door, opened it and told Bo to come in. Standing at the door, Bo took a glance around and sniffed the air, then with trepidation, he gingerly stepped into the house. He sniffed the wrought iron decorations of the antique sewing machine, paying close attention to the pedal. His nose ran all over the machine to the drawers then back down to the pedal.

"That was my great-grandmother's sewing machine. You didn't even need electricity to sew," Allison explained. "The pedal works the needle."

"Interesting," Brendon said. "I've never seen one of these antiques up close. Do you still use it?"

"Oh no! I have an industrial sewing machine at my shop."

Everyone's attention turned to Bo who lifted his snout, taking in more smells of the house, his nose telling him pancakes and bacon had recently been made. He smelled the odor of a fresh shower and the floral scents lingering on Allison's skin. He smelled the sweaty boy, the musty scent of his owner, lemon-scented furniture polish, a stronger cleaner in the kitchen, dish washing soap, hand soap, and a hundred other smells that make a house a home. His nose also told him human pheromones were being released, especially by the female of the house.

Bo went over to Allison, wagged his tail, and nosed her leg.

"Wow!" Brendon said. "I've never seen him do that. He must like you."

"What do I do?" Allison asked. "I've never had a dog."

"Let him sniff your hand. Don't pet him yet."

"He won't bite, will he?"

"No," Brendon said. "He already knows that you're a good person. Bo is a good judge of character. He sure didn't like..." Brendon cut himself of before he badmouthed a customer of Allison's.

"Who didn't he like?" Allison asked.

"Oh, it was nobody...it's not important."

"Who? Tell me?"

"Lee Mercer," Brendon finally divulged.

"Your dog's very smart," Allison said. "I don't like Lee either. Bo is welcome anytime."

"Thank you. Can I get Bo some water? He's probably thirsty."

"Josh, would you do the honors please?" Allison asked.

"On it, Mom."

"Brendon," Allison said, "have a seat at the table. You two must be terribly thirsty. Lemonade is ready."

While Allison set the plastic glasses on the table, Bo gulped water in the kitchen.

"Mom, guess what?"

"What?" Allison asked, pouring lemonade.

"Mr. McMahon doesn't live far from us."

"Actually, I already knew that."

"You did?" Brendon asked. "How?"

"From the address on the receipt."

"Of course." Brendon let out a big breath he had been holding. He turned to Josh, "It's okay to call me Brendon."

"Okay," Josh said, barely able to contain his enthusiasm. "Brendon lives about a mile up the road. He said anytime I wanted to practice throwing I could ride my bike up to his place. Or maybe even ride the go-cart that Dad made me." He took a gulp of lemonade.

"Oh, I don't know about that," Allison said. She stole a look at Brendon. "I'm not sure the go-cart works anymore."

"Brendon said he could fix it."

"I can't trouble him to do that," Allison said.

"Mom!" Josh protested. "Brendon said that if we needed anything–"

"It's something people say to be polite. I doubt if–"

"It's no trouble, none at all," Brendon said. "I'd be happy to take a look at it. It probably only needs some gasoline or a new sparkplug."

After Brendon and Josh finished the lemonade,

Allison walked them to the front door, Bo tagging along. As they headed to the garage, she couldn't help thinking they looked like father and son, and for a moment it was like Doug and Josh were together doing the things father and son should do.

It wasn't that she was even sad or melancholy at the thought; it was something to remember fondly, like her favorite dress that had gotten too small, still hanging in her closet reminding her of good times.

While Brendon and Josh tinkered in the garage, Allison busied herself with minor housework, first sweeping then mopping. She dusted the furniture in the den, gathered dirty clothes and started a laundry load. She took the towels and washcloths from the dryer, set them on the sofa, folding them then setting them on the coffee table to be put up later. After that, she stacked the now dry breakfast dishes in the cupboard and put away the silverware.

With hardly any time elapsed, Allison decided to make a batch of peanut butter cookies. She had all the ingredients necessary. Peanut butter, flour, butter, eggs, baking powder, brown sugar, white sugar, and vanilla. While the oven was preheating, she mixed everything together using her grandmother's recipe with instructions to spoon the tacky batter into little balls onto a cookie sheet spelled 'cooky sheet' in handwritten script. Allison had never bothered to correct the recipe, because the misspelling always brought a smile to her face.

Almost an hour later and with two batches of cookies cooling on wire racks, she decided to check on Brendon and Josh. She opened the door to be greeted by an ungodly hot breeze. It was like opening an oven in her face. She stepped out on the porch and was about to call out to them when a go-cart zoomed out of the garage, bounced along the yard, and skidded to the driveway where it stopped.

"Mom! It works!" Josh yelled. "Brendon got it working. Can I take it for a spin?"

"Only for a little ways. Not far. Be sure your helmet is on tight. Don't go past the creek and don't go too fast! Cookies are ready, too!" Allison yelled back. She stepped off the porch and walked over to Brendon, standing next to him.

Josh waved, floored the pedal, and in a few seconds he was out of sight. Bo barked and ran after him, giving up after a short run. He came back hot and thirsty.

It was quiet. The wind rustled the leaves, and a dragonfly flitted by, landing on a railing before flying away. Bo panted, investigating a scent in the grass.

"I can't believe you got that to work," Allison said. "What did you do?"

"I cleaned the engine and the sparkplug, taped together one of the hoses, and added some gasoline I found in the garage."

"I wouldn't have had a clue on how to do any of that."

"I meant it when I said if you needed anything."

"Thank you."

"Let's get out of the sun," Brendon said. He removed his baseball cap, and ran the back of his hand over his forehead. "Bo, you too. Up here." He motioned for the dog to lie on the porch.

Bo eagerly obeyed and happily loped up to a shady spot on the porch where he promptly plopped down.

"Good idea. Let's sit on the porch steps."

Allison sat with her knees tucked, arms around them. Brendon stretched out his legs, leaned back, and propped one arm on the porch.

Sitting on the steps, they were in close proximity, and both were aware of the intimacy of the porch even though they had a panorama in front of them. The immediate yard was tidy, mowed grass, a green hedge lining the front of the house. Large oaks and pines dotted the land, blue sky as far as the eye could see. A cardinal flitted and chirped in one of the trees, calling to a mate. Other birdsong melodies filled the air: a mockingbird, the steady tap, tap, tap of a woodpecker, field sparrows, meadowlarks, quail.

"So," Brendon pondered, trying to think of something to break the silence. "Your husband must have been quite handy to make the go-cart."

"He was. Doug made it as a birthday present for Josh. He made it so that he and Josh could ride together. They never got to take it for a ride." Allison's gaze drifted away. "Josh misses his dad."

Brendon faced Allison. "I don't think a son ever gets over missing his dad. I still miss mine."

"Oh, I didn't know your dad was gone. I'm sorry."

"Both my parents passed away. My mom back when I was in high school, my dad not long after that." Brendon paused, reached down to the flowerbed and broke off a blade of grass, twirling it between his fingers. "You have a fine son. You should be proud of him."

"I am." Allison turned to meet Brendon's incredibly blue eyes, soulful eyes, ones that had a story to tell, and there was something in the way he looked at her that was different than when other men looked at her. It was like he looked at her like he already knew her.

The sun shined, and a warm breeze floated by, catching Allison's hair, blowing a lock onto her face.

For a long moment, they looked at each other. Allison parted her full lips.

Brendon reached up to push her hair away from her face, and when he touched her face, she closed her eyes, tilting her head into the palm of his strong hand, reveling in his touch. He ran his finger down the side of her face, taking in the curve of her cheeks, the way her lips came together. He looked at her, memorizing her face as if he would never see her again, and it was so natural to be here with her in this moment, yet at the same time it was wrong.

He knew it was wrong.

How could he?

He had already fallen in love with her picture, looking at it repeatedly, and now he was falling quickly for the real woman. She was more beautiful than he had ever imagined.

It was no use fighting the attraction, and he gently ran his fingers over her lips, his hand brushing against her cheeks. Putting his hand behind her neck, he brought her closer until his lips met hers. It was the most natural sensation in the world, and he kissed her long and hard, the way a man should kiss a woman, and she responded. Brendon put his hand around her head, caressing her, running his fingers through her soft hair.

How long they kissed, their hearts beating heavy, they were unsure, and they could have continued, and would have if it hadn't been for the roar of the go-cart and of Bo jumping off the porch.

Allison practically catapulted up from Brendon. Dazed, she looked at him, smoothed her hair and tugged her shirt, checking to make sure everything was covered. Josh rounded the corner in the go-cart, barreled down the driveway, dust and pebbles kicking up behind him. He brought the go-cart to an abrupt stop inches in front of the porch.

"Mom, you look funny."

"No I don't," Allison replied, all the while looking like a kid who got caught with their hands in the proverbial cookie jar.

"What have y'all been doing?" Josh asked.

"Nothing," Allison said. "Talking, that's all."

Brendon stood. "I'd better get going. I've taken up enough of your time." He stole a peek at Allison trying to gauge her reaction.

"What? No," Josh said. He took his helmet off. "You just got here." He turned his attention to Allison. "Mom, didn't you make peanut butter cookies? Let's have some of those."

"I've got things I need to work on at home, Josh. And besides, this is your mom's day off. I don't want to intrude any more than I already have," Brendon said.

"Josh, Brendon needs to go home, and we have chores to do. I'll pack Brendon some cookies to take home. Put the go-cart up for now."

"Okay," Josh huffed. He slapped the helmet on the seat next to him.

"Thanks for stopping by and getting the go-cart running," Allison said, feeling suddenly awkward.

"My pleasure. Anytime. I'm just down the road. The offer still stands if you need anything. And nice meeting you, Josh." Brendon turned, whistled for Bo, and walked toward his truck.

"Hey, wait," Josh said. "I have an idea." He looked at his mom. "Aren't you making hamburgers tonight?"

"That's right."

"And didn't you say you were making extra for dinner tomorrow night?"

"Yes." Allison furrowed her brow, wondering where Josh was going with this conversation. Then it hit her. Right as she was about to shut down Josh he butted in.

"Mom, can Brendon come for dinner tonight?"

Chapter 15

Everyone held their breath, and Allison wasn't quite sure how to answer that question: *Can Brendon come for dinner tonight?*

It wasn't like it was a difficult question to answer, only requiring a simple *yes* or *no*, and she had asked many people that same question. This time was different and she knew it, and from the way Josh's words hung in the air, the way Brendon looked at her, it was obvious that Brendon and Josh were waiting for her lead.

Okay, it was only dinner, not a marriage proposal, right? And how silly was that? Thinking one dinner would lead to marriage or anything else for that matter. They *had* kissed though, and it had been so long since she had been kissed that way.

She was fooling herself.

From the first moment she met him, the way her heart fluttered when he was near, the way her body lit up when their lips touched, she knew Brendon was something special, and she knew he felt it too.

She had promised herself not to get involved with anyone. It would be too confusing to Josh, and suppose things ended badly? Suppose she fell in love with him, only to have him leave her, or worse yet, die like Doug had? How could she even think all those things after knowing the guy for all of one day? She didn't know the first thing about him, like where he was born, what his favorite color was, if he had been married, or even if he had children. Maybe she was overanalyzing.

Can Brendon come for dinner tonight?

"Well, Mom?"

"I guess it's alright," Allison finally answered. "Sure, why not? Brendon, come back at seven and we'll have hamburgers."

"I'd be happy to grill," Brendon offered.

"That'd be great, Mom! Grilled hamburgers! I can't wait. They're so much better than frying them in a skillet. I'll help too."

"Okay, it's settled. Grilled hamburgers it is. I'll even make one for Bo, so he's welcome to come too."

After Brendon and Bo left, Josh put the go-cart in the garage, gathered the baseball gloves and balls, and he and Allison went inside. Josh plopped down on the sofa, put the gloves and baseball in the wicker basket at the end of the sofa, and turned on the TV.

Allison busied herself in the kitchen inventorying the refrigerator, making sure she had all the makings for hamburgers. The lettuce was fresh, tomatoes ripe, pickles crisp. Mayo and mustard were still in date, buns were soft, even cheese was on hand in case anyone wanted a cheeseburger. The watermelon was red and juicy. She had even bought a sack of charcoal impulsively a couple of months ago, thinking about how Doug would grill on Sunday afternoons when their family was whole, when Doug and Madison were still alive.

Brief melancholy washed over her, clouding what had been a perfect day. Standing at the kitchen sink, Allison twirled her locket.

"Mom?"

"What, honey?"

"Do you like Brendon?"

"What do you mean?"

"Are you going to date him?"

"Josh! What kind of question is that?"

"I think it would be cool if you dated him. He likes you."

"How do you know?"

"Mom, you're so lame sometimes. I just know. He's a hundred percent better than that Lee guy." Josh got up from the couch. "I'm going to go to my room. Is that okay?"

"Sure. Don't sleep the day away, though."

The afternoon went quickly. Allison busied herself with cleaning and painting the chest-of-drawers she'd found at a garage sale a couple of weeks ago. It was about waist high, with three drawers and rusty pulls in the shape of a lion. Those had to go, so she had bought crystal-looking Plexiglas pulls that added a nice clean finish. She set out newspaper on the porch, taping the corners down using painters tape so the wind wouldn't blow them around or up on the paint she planned to use.

She dusted and cleaned the corners, taking care to remove all one hundred years of gunk. The process took a good part of the afternoon because Allison was a stickler for details. Satisfied the chest-of-drawers was clean, she found a screwdriver and opened the paint can, stirring it with a stir stick. The paint was supposed to contain primer, so at least she could skip that step. And if the weather cooperated, she'd have the chest-of-drawers painted by evening, then in the morning she'd screw on the new pulls in time to display it at her shop on Monday.

As she worked she couldn't help but to think of Brendon and the kiss they shared. And she couldn't wait for the evening.

Chapter 16

While Allison kept busy, so did Brendon. After he got home, he inventoried the work he needed to do. First there was the sagging barbed-wire fence. Next on the agenda was the gate that had fallen off of its hinges.

Digging around in the toolshed, he found what he needed to repair the gate. Donning a pair of well-used work gloves, he set the box of nails down along with boards he needed. It was hot and dirty manual work, and soon sweat trickled down the sides of his back. He pulled and twisted on rusty nails, loosening them one by one until the rotted boards crumbled away. He hammered new nails in, tested the strength of the boards, working diligently.

While he worked he let his thoughts wander to what Krishna had said. They had been at Brendon's apartment, packing, getting ready for his move.

"Have you thought about what you will say to her?" Krishna asked.

Brendon was taping a box shut. "I have no clue."

"I think when you find her, you'll know what to say."

Brendon set the box aside and began to assemble another one. When he finished, he gathered some books and placed them in the box. "I've tried to imagine what I would say if someone came to me out of the blue and said something like this: I was the policeman who killed your wife."

"What would you do?"

"I'm not sure. Maybe ask them why. Maybe tell them what it had done to me. How it almost destroyed me. Make them feel what I felt."

"Is this a rehearsal for what you plan to say?" Krishna asked.

"Maybe."

"If so, you have a lot of practicing to do."

"You have a better idea?"

"It would be better for you to find a way to meet her, a way that seems natural. Get to know her, let her get to know you. Let her discover the man that you are, and the one you have become. You need to do that before you ask for her forgiveness."

"I don't plan on getting to know her. As soon as I tell her, I know what she'll say. She'll tell me to get lost."

"How can you know that? You haven't even met her."

"I will, and when I do, I'll have to tell her. Even if by some wild stretch of the imagination, she forgives me, do you think she'd have anything to do with me once she finds out I was the one?"

Krishna shrugged. "Nobody knows the answer to that question." He tapped his chest, over his heart. "Only the heart knows these things. The important thing is: Have you forgiven yourself?"

"Maybe. Sometimes. I don't really know."

Brendon wished Krishna had never brought up the subject, knowing it was useless to try to reason with a man who was an impossible romantic, believed in Feng Shui and other invisible forces guiding the stars and the universe. Every action had a reaction, a wrong for a right, black and white, up and down, north and south, east and west, yin and yang.

Yet when Krishna left, Brendon found himself staring at the picture he had printed out, thinking that maybe, Krishna might be right after all.

The afternoon became unbearably hot, and Brendon wiped the sweat from his brow, the sun beating mercilessly on the parched ground. Every once in a while, Bo got up from the depression he had dug under the oak tree, stretched, and dug a little in the ground to find a cooler spot. When he finally stopped digging, Bo stuck his nose in the dirt, huffing twice. He sunk into the coolness.

It was hot and still.

A lone cicada sang a sad song, others joined in gradually, before falling silent. A hot breeze whistled the pines, a grasshopper twittered, and Bo slept fitfully in the heat.

After Brendon finished repairing the gate, he retrieved a string of barbed wire, uncoiled it, and stretched it as tight as he could around a cedar post then pounded nails back into the fence post.

There, one post down, twenty more to go.

He whiled away the afternoon, working his way down the fence, taking breaks from time to time and drinking plenty of water. He learned quickly to stay hydrated, otherwise he'd be socked with a vicious headache that would last the night.

It was a hot day and the sun burned his skin. He took off his cap and mopped the sweat trickling down his brow and into his eyes. He glanced at the brassy sky. There was not a cloud around, and according to the weather reports, there wouldn't be much relief from the heatwave in the near future.

He worked for a little while longer and after he pounded in the last nail, he looked at the fence, satisfied at his handiwork.

Bo stirred, rose, and stretched in the way dogs do. He panted. Even for a dog, the heat was becoming too hot.

"Come on, Bo. Let's go inside and cool off. Time for me to shower and change before heading to Allison's."

Bo didn't have to be told twice. As soon as Brendon turned, Bo happily padded after him into the house.

As promised, Brendon showed up right on time at Allison's house. It was 7 pm, still plenty of light, still plenty hot. By 9, it would be almost dark, and hopefully a little cooler at 90 degrees. At these temperatures, even a few degrees made a big difference. He was wearing loose-fitting jeans and a short sleeved shirt that fell over the waistband of his jeans. His hair had gotten a little long and unruly so he grabbed his favorite baseball cap and threw it on. He'd take it off once he got inside.

He felt a little sheepish when Allison told him not to bring anything other than his appetite and Bo. He did promise to get the fire going and to grill the hamburgers. At least that was something.

Brendon parked his truck and dropped his keys in his pocket, and didn't even have to knock on the door. Josh bounded out the front door and down the steps to greet him. He looked as eager as a kid on Christmas morning.

"Hey, Brendon!"

"Josh." Brendon dipped his chin. "Good to see you again, buddy."

"Mom said I could show you around and where we'll start the fire. She's inside getting the hamburgers seasoned. We don't have much of a grill, only some rocks I put in a circle." Josh talked fast and motioned for Brendon to follow him. "Over here. We'll grill in the backyard. Do you think that's a good place? I already put the rocks in a circle. Do you like how I put the rocks? I learned that in Boy Scouts. Mom said we have to be careful because it's so dry. And look what else I did. I already took the hose and soaked the ground. If you want to, we could throw some balls. I've already got the gloves and balls out. I thought if we—"

"Whoa. Slow down. We're not in a rush. Let's do one thing at a time, okay?" Brendon asked.

"Alright. What should we do first?"

"First, I'm going to say 'Hi' to your mom."

"Oh, yeah, right. She's in the kitchen." Josh turned to the house and yelled at the top of his lungs, "Moooommmm! Brendon's here!"

"Well," Brendon remarked, "I know one thing's for sure. You have a loud voice."

Josh laughed. "That's what Mom says."

"Stay here and play with Bo a minute, would you?"

"Sure."

Walking into the house from the back door, Brendon stepped inside. He removed his baseball cap and set it aside. Allison was standing at the kitchen sink washing tomatoes. The hamburgers had already been molded into patties and seasoned, and were sitting on a platter on the counter.

Allison wiped her hands on a dishtowel. "I was looking at you two from the window. Josh talked your ear off, didn't he?" She cracked a mischievous smile.

"He was telling me all about how he placed the rocks, and about soaking the ground, and—"

Allison broke out laughing.

"What?"

"He's been getting ready all afternoon. You should have seen him. Running around like a chicken with its head cut off, gathering rocks trying to find the right ones, putting them in a circle, removing one, watering the grass. I thought he was going on a date, not me."

"This is a date?" Brendon asked playfully.

"Oh...I...I don't know...I thought so, I mean..." Allison stammered.

"I'd like it to be a date."

Allison reached up to her hair and brushed away a

strand. "Me too." She smoothed her shirt and looked at her pants. "I should have dressed better."

"You look beautiful just the way you are, except for one thing."

"What?"

"That black streak on your forehead," Brendon said. Puzzled, he moved closer to Allison. "What is that?"

"Oh," Allison said touching her forehead. "It must be paint. I've been painting all afternoon, finishing a chest-of-drawers for my shop. I didn't even have time to change."

"Here, let me," Brendon said. He tore off a paper towel, ran some tap water on it and reached up to Allison's forehead. Holding her chin he gently massaged her forehead, wiping away the black paint. It wasn't really a smear, more like a tiny spot, and on her fair complexion, it stood out.

While Brendon dabbed the spot, he was conscious of how close he was to Allison, and of her breaths upon him. The house was quiet, the moment was heady, and if anyone would have told him cleaning someone's face was sexy, he would have told them they were dreaming.

When he finished, he wadded the damp paper towel and set it on the counter. Allison looked at him, holding his long gaze.

He stepped closer to her. "Your forehead is a little red. Let me kiss it to make it feel better." Allison's eyes confirmed her approval, and when Brendon kissed her forehead, she closed her eyes and exhaled a breath she had been holding.

"Here," she said, turning her cheek to the right. "I think you missed a spot."

Brendon obliged, kissing her cheek, then the other one, nibbling her neck before connecting with her lips. He wrapped his arms around her, holding her tight against him, and they kissed long and hard, a kiss meant to express how they felt, and wanted to feel. They stayed pressed against each other until Bo's throaty bark interrupted the sensual moment, as if to warn them they would be having visitors.

Brendon stepped away, followed by the unmistakable sound of the screen door opening. Allison pivoted to the sink and snatched a tomato and a paring knife, pretending to cut something at the sink.

Josh rushed in. "Mom, we need to get the fire going. I'm starving. Do we have anything to eat?"

Turning from the sink, she said, "You can have potato chips if you don't eat too many."

"Okay. Brendon, do you want any?" Josh asked.

"No, I don't eat chips."

"What? Who doesn't eat chips?" Josh asked. He grabbed a sack of potato chips, pulled it open, and shoved a potato chip to Brendon's mouth. "Have one."

Brendon flinched, and his tone was gruff when he said, "No. Like I said, I don't eat chips."

Allison noticed Brendon's change in demeanor. "Joshua!" Allison said in her best warning tone. "Brendon said he doesn't eat potato chips. You don't force anyone to eat anything. Ever."

"I was just joking around."

"That was not polite." Allison narrowed her eyes, lowered her voice. "Apologize. Now."

"Okay." Josh scowled. "I'm sorry."

"No harm done." Brendon said, stealing a look at Allison. "Tell you what, Josh, let's you and me gather some wood and get the fire going. Is that alright, Allison?"

"Yes, absolutely."

Brendon and Josh gathered dry wood for the fire, including smaller twigs and leaves to start it with, then larger kindling once the fire had caught. To ensure the

119

fire would be contained in the rocks, Brendon directed Josh to get a rake to brush away any dry pine needles or leaves too close to the fire. As a further precaution, he told Josh to turn on the hose and wet the ground even more than he already had that afternoon.

Once the kindling had turned to embers, Brendon set the grill over the fire, letting it get hot before putting on the hamburger patties. He told Josh to let his mother know it would only take minutes to grill the patties.

Bo staked himself a spot near where Brendon grilled, waiting for a wayward hamburger to fall on the ground. The aroma of freshly grilled hamburgers filled the air and when Josh was in the house doing something, Brendon scooped up a hamburger, cut it using a metal spatula then blew on it to cool it down. He slipped it to Bo.

Bo gobbled it up, along with a leaf. The extra bit of roughage didn't appear to bother him.

Since a half-eaten hamburger would be suspicious, Brendon generously gave the other half to Bo. "No more begging. Understand?"

Bo woofed once and wagged his tail.

Almost on cue, Josh and Allison stepped out of the house holding plates and utensils, freshly cut watermelon, condiments, and drinks.

"I thought we'd eat outside," Allison said. "It's such a nice night. Stars are coming out. Let's set everything on the patio table."

The meal went quickly, and by the time they had finished, stars shined brightly in the night sky. Josh said he was getting sleepy so asked to be excused. "Take Bo inside, too," Allison instructed, "and put down a blanket for him in the den." Brendon helped Allison clear the table and took the bowls into the kitchen, setting them in the sink.

He then retrieved a couple of lawn chairs from the garage and set them side by side in the backyard.

It was quiet. Somewhere a whippoorwill chanted, an owl hooted in the distance, and a nocturnal animal scurried in the dry underbrush.

"Isn't the sky beautiful?" Allison commented. "I never appreciated the stars in Houston, or could even see them for that matter."

"Too many lights," Brendon said. "You'd be lucky to see a full moon."

"I bought a book on stars the other day," Allison said.

"What for?"

"To learn more about them."

"Is it a new hobby of yours?" Brendon asked.

"Not really." Allison turned to Brendon. "Something my daughter said before she died piqued my interest, although I've never quite understood it."

Brendon was curious, but he didn't want to pry. "I can't imagine what it must be like to lose a child. I'm so sorry." He reached over and offered his hand for comfort. Allison took it and threaded her fingers through his.

"I'm getting to the point where I can think about Madison without crying." She looked to the heavens. "There's something peaceful about looking at stars, don't you think?"

"I never thought about it that way, but I suppose so."

"So many millions of stars, twinkling their magic. I can understand why early people romanticized them. All the mystery, wondering what they were, no science to explain them."

For a while, Brendon and Allison sat side by side, holding hands as they looked at the stars in the dark sky.

"Children have the most incredible imaginations," Allison said after a long silence, "especially when they are little. Or maybe it's because their minds are so pure

121

they are able to see things differently than adults. Right before Madison died she told me to *look to the stars.*" Allison shifted in the chair. "What do you think that means?"

Brendon shrugged. "I don't know. Maybe she was trying to tell you something. Maybe she liked stars. Maybe they wanted you to see them in heaven with the stars." Brendon removed his hand from Allison's and reached over to her. He brought his hand to the locket she always wore. "Like this locket for example. The way the diamond is set looks like a star."

Allison brought her hand up and touched his hand.

"Stars always shine," Brendon said. "Perhaps it was her way of telling you that her memory would always stay alive."

"I've never even thought of it that way," Allison said.

For a while, they sat there in silence, each with their own thoughts, and when Josh let Bo out of the house, Brendon took that as his clue it was time for him to leave. Even though it was only 11 pm, he really didn't want to go. He wanted to sit under the stars forever with Allison, talking. Reluctantly, he got up, stretched, and said it was time for him to go. He thanked Allison for a wonderful evening.

"I'd like to do this again."

"Me too," she replied.

After Brendon and Bo left, Allison locked the house and checked on Josh. He was too old for a good night kiss, though she did tiptoe into his room and tuck the covers into the bed.

Tidying up in the kitchen, she mused on the evening with Brendon. She wasn't sure what to even call him. A boyfriend? A friend? Their relationship was so new and really, they hadn't even gone out in public, only this normal evening, grilling and talking, hanging around the fire like they were a family.

Allison longed to have a complete family with a husband, and she was still young enough to have more children, not that she thought about that often. Having another child wouldn't replace Madison, nor would that be a reason to have another child.

She wasn't nervous in Brendon's presence, yet she didn't know the first thing about him. Why had he left Houston? He mentioned briefly he had been on the police force, yet when she asked what she thought were innocuous questions, he dodged any direct answers and deftly changed the subject. Maybe he had some bad memories he didn't want to re-hash. Allison knew all about bad memories.

He didn't seem like he was withholding any deep, dark secret, yet there was a reticence about him she couldn't quite put her finger on. Weren't all guys like that? They didn't talk about their feelings, or openly show emotion. They'd rather talk about their favorite sports' teams, or work, golf, politics, things she had no interest in.

Theirs was a chance meeting, two people from different backgrounds, finding each other in this big, wide world. What would be the chances of meeting someone in a small town? She didn't know the population of Houston, assuming it must have been over two million people. Bastrop? Probably around seven thousand total, maybe a little more in the entire county. The chances of meeting her Mr. Right were astronomical, and perhaps *that's* what Madison had meant by, 'look to the stars'.

Her thoughts were interrupted by a knock at the door.

Silly Brendon. He must have forgotten something.

Chapter 17

While Allison, Brendon, and Josh were having a friendly dinner, Lee Mercer had been fuming the entire day.

He had been sitting in his favorite lazy chair, nursing a bottle of whiskey, watching an old western. Well, not really watching, he had it on as background noise and wasn't paying any attention to it because nothing could take his mind off of Mr. Hotshot and that mangy dog who had ruined what had been the start of a perfectly good morning. Lee cracked a smile thinking about Crystal and their little early morning romp. Despite the fact he had to drop a few Benjamins, it was worth it.

Early that morning when he stopped at Brendon's house, all Lee was doing was trying to be neighborly. To say hello and welcome the guy to country living.

And what kind of thanks did he get? A bite by a mangy dog, some old country cur not even worth the time of day. When he went to teach the dog some manners, Mr. Hotshot called him on it. If the guy hadn't looked like he meant business and had the muscle, Lee would have showed him a thing or two, like how his boot looked up close, or better yet, how dirt looked and smelled when his face was smashed into it.

Then there was Brendon's cool voice, the same *don't-mess-with-me* tone of voice that Lee used to intimidate people. The same authoritative voice police used, a voice used to render people to shivering blobs of blubber. Who did the guy think he was? The law? Lee scoffed at the thought. He recognized that tone of voice alright, except nobody had ever challenged him, so when Brendon said *I wouldn't do that if I was you* Lee was caught off guard. When Lee used that voice, people backed away and stood down from him. It was exactly what Brendon had made Lee do.

Oh, he hated that guy. Nobody told Lee what to do.

Then there was the matter of Allison. Thinking about her made Lee act bat-shit crazy, lose his cool, and made him lose sleep. And Lee liked his nap time, which was what he had done all afternoon. The last time any woman made Lee lose sleep was when his 15 year old girlfriend told him she was pregnant. Lee was 18 at the time, and no way was some two-bit teenage slut going to mess up his life. Dumb bitch. A few well-placed punches took care of *that* problem.

After Lee woke up from his afternoon siesta, he stumbled over to the bathroom and took a shower. His mouth tasted like a rat's nest so he gargled several times, swished his mouth around with mouthwash, then checked his pearly whites. He put his hand to his mouth, huffed a breath, and sniffed it. Passable.

Time to swing by Allison's place.

Lee had stopped by the grocery store earlier that day and bought an apple pie and a pint of ice-cream. No need to buy a gallon, it would be wasted on that kid. A pint would do.

He raced down the country road, apple pie and ice-cream sitting on the passenger seat in a plastic bag. He checked his watch. 8 pm. By now, she would have finished with dinner, and seeing that Lee was a gentleman and all, he wouldn't be intruding on dinner time. The last time he was invited to a home-cooked dinner, his date had asked him to help clean up. He begrudgingly helped, then when it was time for her to put out, she showed him the door. Lee learned a valuable lesson that day, which was to come over *after* dinner. No dishes for Lee. That was womenfolk work.

Lee came up to Allison's house and when he was about to swing his truck into the driveway he couldn't believe his eyes. "What the crap!" he blurted out loud.

Mr. Hotshot's truck was parked in front of her house.

Didn't that beat all? First he got bit by that mangy cur then the guy moved in on his girl. *His* girl.

Lee's imagination ran wild, thinking about Allison and Brendon in bed, doing the dirty, their sweaty bodies grinding against each other. Moaning. For hours.

He couldn't stand the thought.

He threw the gear into reverse, gunned the engine, and peeled out of there. He lost all track of time, driving down unmarked country roads, dust and rocks flying in the air, then to another road, and finally out to the main highway.

He banged his hands on the steering wheel and screamed a whole slew of obscenities, but without anyone listening, it wasn't as satisfying. For several hours he drove along the winding highway, up and down hills, swerving in and out of lanes when he decided to go back to Allison's to give her a piece of his mind.

He made an illegal U-turn in the median.

Seconds later, screaming sirens and flashing lights clued Lee into the fact he needed to pull over. Damn cops. Lee pulled over and rolled the window down, clicking on the dome light. It had gotten dark, and he knew that cops didn't like to come up to a dark car. Now wasn't that smart of him? Light the dome light for the man in blue? Or maybe khaki in this case. And if the guy wasn't wearing khaki, Lee would be in deep doo-doo. Lee and the sheriff were friends, and friends watch each other's back. Lee would let the officer pulling him over know all about his long-time relationship with the Bastrop sheriff.

Lee planned on using his best good 'ole boy, back-slapping, high-fiving persona to talk his way out of a ticket. Not to mention he had a few leftover bills in his wallet.

While the trooper stood outside the truck and Lee pretended to look for his driver's license, several Benjamins just happened to pop up their lovely green faces where the trooper could see.

The trooper was new and not impressed or informed regarding the good 'ole boy local network, so he ordered Lee out of the car and gave him a field sobriety test. Lee squeaked by. The trooper lectured Lee and slapped him with several violations including speeding, an illegal U-turn, threw in an expired inspection sticker, and Lee ended up with a mighty hefty fine.

And it was all Allison's fault.

If she hadn't been hooking-up...and what self-respecting woman does the dirty on the Sabbath? Lee became angrier.

After the trooper left, Lee hightailed it out of there and headed straight to Allison's house. Trying to keep his speed under the speed limit aggravated him even more, so by the time he got to her house, he was hopping mad.

Allison was about to finish the dishes when there was a knock at the door, thinking Brendon must have forgotten something. In her bedtime clothes of a loose fitting shirt and shorts, she rushed to the door without bothering to turn on the hallway light. The house was dark. Forgetting her normal *who's there* security question or checking to see who was on the front porch, she applied her best wide smile and swung open the door expecting to see Brendon.

Her smile quickly disappeared. "Lee?" Allison asked incredulously. "What are you doing here?"

"I came to see you."

"What? It's after eleven. Have you been drinking?" His eyes were vacant and mean, and a chill captured her.

"As a matter of fact I have been. Guess what? I got stopped by the DPS." Lee glared at Allison. "It's all your fault. I did pass the field sobriety test the DPS officer made me take."

"*My* fault?" Allison furrowed her brow. "That's ridiculous. You're drunk and need to leave." When she tried to slam the door shut Lee stuck his boot in the door jamb.

"Not so fast, little lady." He pushed past Allison and stormed into the house. His eyes roamed over the kitchen and den. "Just you and the boy here?"

Allison remained quiet.

"Guess that answers my question."

"What do you want?" Allison demanded. She had never seen Lee like this, acting maniacally, and her instincts told her to be wary. She backed up, putting the kitchen table between them.

"You," Lee said as if he was a predator zeroing in on his meal.

"You're scaring me. I'm asking you again to leave."

"Oh," Lee said, mocking. "I'm not good enough for you but Mr. Hotshot is?"

"What are you talking about?"

"Don't play coy with me," Lee snapped. He took a fast step around the table and came face to face with Allison. "You were here with him. I know what you were doing."

"We weren't doing anything." Allison threw her shoulders back in a show of defiance. "I don't need to explain anything to you. He's a friend and a customer."

"Providing a little extra customer service? Huh?"

"I won't dignify that with an answer." Allison nervously glanced around, and flicked on the kitchen light. "Look, Lee, there's never been anything between us. I thought I'd made that clear. And as of now, you're no longer welcome."

"We'll see about that," Lee said. He flipped the kitchen light off, plunging the kitchen and living area into darkness. The outside porch light cast dark shadows into the house.

Lee cornered Allison, pushing her back up against the sink. When she tried to pull away from him, Lee caught her and pinned her arms behind her. "I'll show you what you've been missing."

"No, Lee. Stop. My son's here. Please don't." She tried not to sound scared, tried to keep her voice from wavering.

"Then maybe you need to shut up and do as I say."

Allison thought about screaming for help, but dismissed that idea because Josh was no match for Lee, and Lee might actually hurt her son.

A weapon?

What could she use?

She scanned the counter and sink, and when she spied a heavy cast iron skillet in the sink, she knew what she had to do.

She kneed Lee in the family jewels, he grunted and immediately bent over, releasing his grip on her hands.

She pivoted and reached for the heavy cast iron skillet. Holding it tight, she spun around.

Lee was too fast. He jumped her and grabbed her hand holding the handle of the cast iron skillet. He squeezed hard. Allison cried out in pain and strained against the hold he had on her. Lee squeezed harder.

"Stop, or I'll break your hand."

Lee's voice was gruff, and Allison knew he meant it.

Her hand went limp and Lee removed the skillet, slid it on the floor, and kicked it to the side.

She cringed at Lee's hot breath on her neck, and winced at the touch of his rough hand sliding up under her shirt. Allison gritted her teeth, closed her eyes tight, recoiling in disgust from his touch. She turned away, steeling herself for the worst.

A low voice said, "I wouldn't do that if I was you."

Lee immediately recognized that phase and intonation. He whipped around keeping a death grip on Allison.

"Let her go," Brendon said, glaring at Lee. "Now."

Lee didn't move.

Brendon took a step closer and pushed Allison aside as Lee threw a punch. Brendon pivoted to the side and the force of Lee's swing was so powerful that the momentum caused his weight to shift.

Brendon saw his chance and his left hand made contact with Lee's rib cage. Something cracked.

Lee grunted and doubled over, swinging wildly again.

Brendon blocked the blow and immediately followed through with a right uppercut to Lee's chin.

Lee's swagger diminished into a stagger, and he fought to regain his composure, letting his building rage guide his next action. He reached for his clip-it knife in his front pocket, flicking it open. With a well-placed kick, Brendon knocked the knife away, and it clanged to the floor, sliding out of Lee's reach.

Allison stood at a safe distance, eyes wide. She bent down and crawled on the kitchen floor, searching for her cast iron skillet. She found it and stood up, holding the heavy skillet with both hands as if she was a baseball player holding a bat, ready to hit a homerun.

Brendon came in quickly, smashing a solid right into Lee's stomach. Lee staggered backwards and grunted in pain as he fell into the sofa, knocking it askew.

A wicker basket tumbled to the floor, magazines and papers scattered about the room.

A lamp toppled over.

Brendon pushed forward and shoved Lee with both hands, sending him stumbling into the wall. Lee panted and drew a hand over his mouth, his expression one of pure rage. He lowered his head and lunged at Brendon.

Brendon caught him and with several powerful hits to the body, dropped him in the middle of the floor.

"Had enough?" Brendon asked, towering over Lee.

Lee rolled over on his back and glared at Brendon.

"Get out of here and don't come back."

Rising, Lee steadied himself, leaning over on one knee. His breaths were short and fast. "We'll finish this later." He got up, brushed off his shirt for show, and shot a death stare at Allison, who was still holding the skillet over her head.

"Like I said, get out."

Brendon watched him leave then promptly locked the door. He turned to Allison, whose eyes were wide with fear. "You can put that down now," he said gently. She didn't answer. He walked over to her, nudging the heavy skillet out of her hands. "You're trembling," he said, taking her into his arms, holding her close. He stroked her hair, telling her she was safe now. "Everything's okay. I'm here now." He pulled back and looked Allison straight in the eyes. "Are you injured? Did he hurt you?"

"No." Allison's voice was barely audible.

"We have to report this," Brendon said.

"What? No. I can't embarrass my son."

"Allison," Brendon said, "there's nothing to be ashamed of. He tried to rape you."

"But he didn't."

"He almost did. Allison, you owe it to yourself."

"No, I won't go to the police, and that's final." Allison put her hand to her face. "I don't know what I would have done if you hadn't come back. Thank God you came back. Why did you come back?"

"I forgot my favorite baseball cap. It's over there on the end table."

Allison looked in that direction and laughed nervously. "They're a lousy team. Right now, though, they're my World Series champions."

Josh stumbled out of his bedroom and walked into the den, rubbing the sleep out of his eyes. "What's going on? And who was making all that noise? I thought I heard Mr. Mercer's voice."

"Everything is okay now," Allison said. "You can go back to bed."

"What's wrong, Mom? You look like you've seen a ghost." Josh glanced at Brendon then back to his mom, taking in the disarray of the den. "Was there a fight?" He turned his attention to Brendon, and breathlessly asked, "Did you fight Mr. Mercer?"

"You could say we had a little scuffle."

"A little scuffle! From the looks of it, you whooped his ass!"

"*Joshua!*" Allison gasped. "Don't talk like that."

Josh walked over to Brendon and raised his hand in a high five gesture. He slapped hands with Brendon. "It's about time somebody put that jerk in his place. Did you give him a black eye? What'd he do?" Josh made some mock fighting moves with his fists.

"Josh, that's enough." Allison walked over to Josh and rumpled his hair. "Listen to me. Don't ever let Lee Mercer into the house, do you understand me?"

"Sure, Mom. If he comes back here, I'll whoop his ass too!"

"Go back to bed."

"Good job, Brendon," Josh said. "You're okay in my book."

After Josh went back to bed, Brendon made Allison a cup of hot chocolate. Sitting at the kitchen table, Allison sipped the frothy drink.

"A little bit of sugar helps take the edge off of things."

"I'll remember that the next time you two get in a fight," Allison said. She took a spoon and twirled the drink, clinking the sides.

"What's the history between you and Lee?" Brendon asked.

Allison sighed long and heavy, twirling the gold locket. "When I first moved here, Lee helped me move some heavy furniture. He was driving down the road when he saw me and Josh struggling with the curio cabinet, the one over there in the corner," she said, pointing in the direction of the cabinet. "Josh and I couldn't lift it and since he could, I accepted his help. He stayed for a while and I offered him something to drink, and he didn't seem like he wanted to leave, so I put him to work unpacking things, breaking down boxes, things like that. He told me all about his deceased wife, his kids that were away in college, how he was alone. Plus he had to put his wife's dog to sleep and—"

"He told me the same thing about his wife's dog. Some little white fluffy dog named Butterball. He was lying about what happened." Brendon shook his head in disgust. "There's no telling what he did with that poor dog."

"That's horrible." Allison took another sip of hot chocolate and swallowed loudly.

"After that, he kept coming over and offering to fix things, like the drippy faucet in the bathroom my landlord never repaired. I made him dinner once, and we went out a couple of times, he met me for lunch, a dinner another time. After that I told him I only wanted to be friends. He apologized if he had done anything to upset me, and I told him he hadn't, although he had."

"What did he do?" Brendon asked.

"He tried..." She glanced down. "I wasn't ready to date anyone so soon after Doug died. I was wasting my time with Lee because I knew there wasn't any future with him. He wouldn't take 'no' for an answer. He said he'd give me time and not bother me."

"Did he?"

"For a while he did, then he started coming around more to my store asking me to repair his jeans, or to take them up, oh, I don't know." Allison waved her arms in the air. "He always made up an excuse to see me." She finished the rest of the hot chocolate and took the cup to the sink. "At the July 4th county fair I planned to tell him I didn't want to see him again. Since people would be around I thought it would be a safe place."

"How long have you been scared of him?"

"Is it that obvious?" Allison asked.

"Yes," Brendon said. "When I met you the other day at your shop, I saw Lee in there. I couldn't help noticing your body language when he was close to you."

Allison stepped back to the table and sat down. She shivered. "He gives me the creeps. There's something...wrong with him."

"He's a jerk, and a dangerous one. Don't ever be alone with him."

"I won't."

"For the time being, I'm going to stay here tonight."

"I can't ask you to do that."

"You're not asking. I'll sleep on the couch to make sure you and Josh are safe."

"Thank you," Allison said. "Let me get you a couple of blankets and a pillow."

"Uh, there's one thing, though," Brendon said.

Allison cocked her head. "Yes?"

"Bo is still in the truck. Can he come in too?"

"Absolutely."

Chapter 18

"From the looks of it you had an interesting night," Susan drawled. "You look like you didn't get a wink of sleep."

It was Monday morning, and Allison was in her shop arranging flowers in a vase she planned to put on her newly painted chest-of-drawers to showcase it.

"Brendon spent the night with me."

"Oh?" Susan immediately perked up. "This is better than a strong cup of coffee. I'm wide awake now."

"It's not like that," Allison said.

Susan slumped down in the sofa. "And here I thought I was going to live vicariously through you. Well, what happened?"

Allison explained Sunday's events, beginning with Brendon stopping by in the morning, then how she had invited him to grill hamburgers for dinner, how he and Josh got along so well, how they talked the night away. When she got to the part about Lee trying to force himself on her, Allison had to take a deep breath.

"I can't believe he tried to do that to you!" Susan exclaimed. "It's disgusting. You should report Lee to the authorities."

"I'm not going to. He's in bed with every politician around here, not to mention the sheriff's office, and no one would believe me or Brendon."

"Allie, watch out for him and tell Brendon to also."

For the first time in a long time, Allison felt genuine concern for another man. She remembered their day together, feeling safer than she had in a long time. They had laughed, kissed, held hands, had a wonderful day, and when it ended, she had wistfully watched him leave. She wanted to know more about him, what he wanted to do with his life, why he had left Houston to come back home. Every so often, he had a look in his eyes like he was dealing with things in his past he wasn't quite ready to share. She wondered if something had happened to him on the police force to make him resign or if there had been a tragedy in his childhood. He had mentioned a sister who died young, and when he hesitated to share any more details, Allison let it go. So many things to know, and if they were to have a future together, she'd want to know everything.

During the next week, Brendon and Allison spent a lot of time together, some of it alone, some of it with Josh, and Allison openly showed her affection toward Brendon in front of Josh. There was no need to hide anything, especially since Josh and Brendon got along so well together.

On Wednesday, Brendon made a sack lunch and brought it to Allison, and even though it was against her policy to close the store during lunch, she placed the *Be back in an hour* sign in the front window with the big hand pointing to one o'clock. She and Brendon skipped out of the store, acting like teenagers sneaking away from their parents. They breezed along the sidewalk, rounded the back of the buildings and headed to the banks of the Colorado River, then took a short walk down a steep, grassy embankment. In the park, children played under the watchful supervision of their parents, couples walked hand-in-hand on the sidewalk while others volleyed balls in the tennis court.

Music trickled down from the restaurant on the hill overlooking the river, and Brendon and Allison sat on a blanket while they ate lunch, serenaded by the music.

"Peanut butter and jelly sandwiches are my favorite," Allison teased.

"Homemade with the finest of ingredients. In fact," Brendon said, "I bet you'd like to know that the jelly comes from a quaint little store in town, Sew Good to See You."

Allison laughed.

"I forgot you bought jelly the other day. It's made from grapes I picked along the road."

"You're a woman of many talents."

"What else do you have in here?" Allison asked. She rummaged around inside the shopping bag and pulled out cheese and crackers, then a container of fresh cherries. "I love cherries, especially when they are in season." She popped one in her mouth, savoring the bursting flavor before surreptitiously discarding the pit.

On Thursday, Brendon came over to Allison's house, bringing a new set of baseballs for Josh. At times, Josh purposely threw a grounder out of reach of Brendon so Bo could go fetch it. The only downside was a slobbery ball Bo reluctantly gave up.

They played outside while Allison prepared a summer dinner of Caprese salad, made with fresh mozzarella cheese, spinach, home-grown tomatoes, fresh basil, and bacon cooked in a cast iron skillet, all drizzled with a balsamic glaze and olive oil.

"You can cook bacon in the microwave," Brendon commented. "It saves time."

"It doesn't taste as good as cooking it in a skillet," Allison explained.

Brendon crunched a slice of perfectly cooked bacon. "You're right about that."

When Brendon and Allison were deep in conversation, Josh slipped Bo a piece of bacon.

After dinner, they all moved to the den where they played Texas Hold'em, a popular poker game Allison never could understand. Brendon explained the rules many times, and they played several practice games. After a while, they decided to play Go Fish.

On Friday when Allison came home, she found Brendon caulking the windows. For a moment when he looked at her, she could have sworn Doug was looking at her. Maybe an angel had come from Heaven in the form of Brendon to be a part of her and Josh's life. Sitting in the car, a bag of groceries on the front seat, Allison paused and her fingers went to the gold locket containing Madison's picture. Twirling it, she smiled, thinking about happy times when Doug and Madison were still living. Doug would have wanted her to go on, to live her life, and not be sad.

Allison cherished the memories she had made with Doug, and when it was dark and quiet, she took them out of mental storage, unwrapping them like they were a precious curio to reminisce about.

She concluded her life was here now, making new memories with Brendon, and she realized how content she was. She had worked hard to build a new life for herself and Josh, and now Brendon had come into the picture. As he caulked the windows, standing there on a ladder, his shirt sticking to him, forearms glistening from perspiration, she realized she loved him. And, she thought he loved her too. They had never spoken the words to one another, but his actions said everything that needed to be said.

The days passed, June came and went, sleepy times, hot times with temperatures climbing to 100 degrees, and sometimes surpassing it.

July roared in, sizzling, hot, burning like an overheated car radiator.

Today was the Fourth of July and everyone complained about the heat and lack of rain, and locals wished and prayed for rain.

The weather forecasters all said the same thing: no relief in sight from the unrelenting drought. Locals had "rain parties" where they partied for rain, barbequed and drank, using it as an excuse to get together.

Everything was drooping or dying from the lack of rain, especially the pine trees. The tips of the needles turned brown, a sure sign that the tree was distressed or even dying. Pine trees needed water and lots of it. Even the mighty Colorado River that ran through the entire width of Texas, finally emptying into the Gulf of Mexico, was becoming stagnant. Mud islands began forming in the usually full river, water that kept the Lost Pines nourished.

Even though her electricity bill was higher than normal, Allison kept her store cool for the comfort of her customers. She set up a help-yourself lemonade stand outside of her store in the hopes it would attract and entice tourists into her shop. She was always trying new marketing ideas to attract more customers. She set Dixie cups next to the large see-through plastic thermos filled with ice with lemon slices floating on top. For those who didn't want lemonade, she had plain ice water. Another ice-water filled pitcher contained zesty orange slices for an added cooling touch. It worked, and all throughout June, she had kept busy with a steady flow of customers.

For the Fourth of July sale, Allison also stocked her store with new items she thought might sell well, homemade items and bright artwork that was hers, images of the countryside that she had seen on her walks or drives. She painted close-ups of sunflowers and butterflies, and at times let Josh add his own touches of bugs and caterpillars. Picture frames were usually bought at a flea market or garage sales then later cleaned or painted to match whichever artwork she planned to put in it.

Allison painted each scene twice, keeping track of what was selling so she could discern the pieces selling the best. It wasn't hard, especially since Josh had learned how to work Excel so he could track sales. He kept tabs on all sorts of essential data like the day of the week, the time it sold, who bought it, their age, whether or not a man or woman bought it. He even made note of where it was in the store. She would try something for a day or two, and if it wasn't selling she'd place it somewhere else in the store, perhaps right when the customer walked in, where it would catch their eye.

At home she grew geraniums from cuttings, impatiens, begonias, and when she had time, she had several milkweed plants she grew specifically for monarch butterfly caterpillars. Children were especially fascinated by the yellow and black striped caterpillars that devoured the host plant, as they should since milkweed was the only host plant for the monarch caterpillar.

Several shiny, emerald green chrysalises dotted with tiny gold flakes had attached themselves to specially-made enclosures, covered with netting.

The circle of life she thought, taking a month from when the tiny egg hatched to becoming a beautiful butterfly. Short enough to capture the attention of children and adults alike. Once the caterpillar spun the chrysalis, she'd mist it often during the day to keep it moist. The air-conditioning in the store kept the humidity levels low, and she knew this was not good for the forming butterfly.

"What time can I pick you up tonight?" Brendon asked, holding the cell phone to his ear. He had visited

Allison's store earlier in the day, but due to the number of customers, hadn't gotten a chance to talk to her.

"I'm still here at the store," Allison replied. "It's been so busy today, I haven't even thought about closing up yet."

"Is Josh with you, or would you like me to swing by your house and pick him up?"

"No need, he's still here. Let's meet around eight at the fair?"

"Sounds good. I'll see you soon."

Chapter 19

Brendon estimated the crowd at the county fair to be about two hundred people. Mothers and fathers, grandparents, kids running around and waving hands in the air while being chased by friends with imaginary weapons.

It was 8 pm and still hot, with humidity so high you could practically swim in it.

The waters of the nearby Colorado River gurgled. A fallen cottonwood tree floated down the river, keeping pace with the current.

Bastrop had been built on the banks of the Colorado River, a wide and undulating river, one that back in the heyday of river boat captains and steamboats was a busily traveled thoroughfare.

In current times, locals used the river for fishing and lazy picnics on the banks and for canoe trips.

Brendon immediately picked Allison out of the crowd.

She slowly made her way to the dais where members of the band were milling around during their break. Allison stepped up to the platform, wiggled past the microphone and musical instruments, greeting everyone she knew.

Lee Mercer was on stage doing double duty as the band's guitar and violin player and when needed, vocalist. He eyed over Allison, mentally undressing her.

Allison ignored his sneers.

Brendon wanted to slug the guy.

In the dimming sunlight, twinkling lights strung across the dance area made it romantic. An unexpected breeze came through and Allison's blonde hair swayed in the wind. She reached up and tucked some wispy ends behind an ear. Then Josh came running up and although Brendon couldn't hear the conversation, it was obvious her son's attention was elsewhere.

Allison sent Josh to join his friends to go get a hotdog or popcorn, or anything that boys might like.

As Brendon watched her, he became aware of the longing to be a part of her family. Josh was a great kid, with a great attitude and natural athletic ability, and reminded Brendon of himself when he was that age. Josh was almost like a little brother he could mentor, and they had already bonded over baseball.

When Brendon first came to Bastrop, he was like one of those cellophane wrapped clay cubes found at art stores: hard, cold, and stiff to the touch. Lately, and he wasn't sure when it started, it was as though warm hands were molding him into something pliable, something totally different than he was before. Things that were important to him in the past held no meaning anymore. The criminals he apprehended seemed like a lifetime ago, and the shooting, well, it was a bad memory.

God, he felt invigorated!

It had to be because of Allison. He realized that he had fallen in love with her.

She had on a white cotton peasant blouse with a ruffled scooped neckline. A brown sash belted over a long flowery skirt finished off her attire. The ensemble shouted to the world her femininity and confidence, and Allison flowed like a graceful ballet dancer doing pirouettes across a stage.

He worried about telling her the real reason he had come to Bastrop, that their meeting wasn't happenstance, rather it had been carefully planned.

Would she tell him to get lost? Curse him?

Ask him why he took her husband away from her, ripping a father from a son? Every time he thought he would tell her, words failed him. Falling in love with Allison changed his well-thought out plans of telling her what had happened. What was he going to do now? He couldn't bear the thought she might hate him. He pushed those questions to the back of his mind to be dealt with at a later time because tonight, he'd tell Allison he loved her.

The county fair was situated around the three-story brick courthouse. Cars were parked bumper to bumper in every available parking space, and different types of music wafted from nearby restaurants. Vendors of every imaginable ware had open, walk-in white canvas tents where they displayed mostly handmade items such as jewelry, wooden boxes, sculptures, artwork, metalwork, canned jams and jellies, greeting cards–all inexpensive items that sold well.

The fairgrounds were demarcated by a square of streets surrounding the county courthouse. Yellow and black barricades had been set up to block the flow of traffic so children could play unsupervised in and around the streets and lawn of the county courthouse square.

It was noisy.

Brendon walked over to Allison and put his arms around her. "You look beautiful."

"Thank you."

"Where's Josh?"

"He's playing with some friends."

"Let's go get a glass of wine."

Brendon reached for Allison's hand and picked his

way through the crowd to where a local winery was set up in one of the white canvas tents. Several bottles of their finest Hill Country Texas wine were displayed. He handed over a ten to the store owner behind the counter. Brendon took two of the plastic cups filled with wine, giving one to Allison.

"I propose a toast," he said, holding the cup.

"I'm listening," Allison said.

"To many more days ahead together."

"I like that," Allison said. She took a sip of wine. "You're a puzzle, Brendon McMahon, with some missing pieces."

"What piece are you looking for?" he asked. He took a swallow of wine.

"Let's sit over here," Allison said, motioning to a table next to an oak tree, "where it's a little quieter."

Brendon held the chair for Allison while she sat down. Taking a seat next to her, he took several sips of wine, preparing himself for what she might ask. He wouldn't lie to her–that much he was certain about.

"Why did you leave Houston?" Allison asked.

Relieved that's all Allison wanted to know, Brendon took a deep breath before explaining how he had been at a crossroads in his life. He had been dumped by his fiancée, and was questioning his choice of career. He told her about his increasing nightmares, and when she pressed him about the reasons, he became quiet.

"Whatever it is, you can tell me," Allison said. "I'm here for you."

"I'm not sure I'm ready to talk about it." He abruptly washed down his glass of wine then got up to get another one. When Brendon returned, he sat down and told Allison he left the force just before qualifying for a detective position.

"I don't understand," Allison said. "Why would you quit when you were about to qualify? Isn't that what police officers strive for?"

"I quit because of the shooting."

"What shooting?"

"Allison," Brendon said, "I'm not sure how to tell you this."

She put a hand on his arm. "I know you've been reluctant to share things about your past, but I really want to know."

Brendon hung his head. He explained how he made it a point to stop in at a corner store that had been the target of robberies. On that particular day, the store owner had accidentally tripped, spilling a red slushy on his uniform. Knowing he couldn't report to duty like that, he had gone into the men's room to clean up. "After I cleaned up, I walked out of the bathroom and stumbled in on an armed robbery. Before I could do or say anything the man shot me. Twice. I nearly died."

"I had no idea." Allison took a sip of wine, steeling herself for what she needed to tell Brendon. "My husband died while he was robbing a store. I really have no idea why he would do that. It was so out of character for him."

"I'm so sorry," Brendon said. He put a hand on hers. He treaded into uncharted territory. "Do you hate the policeman who shot him?"

She thought about that before answering. "How did you know a policeman shot him?"

"I...I assumed." Brendon looked at her blankly. He repeated his question. "Do you hate the policeman?"

"Hate is a strong word. I'm not sure I've come to terms with how I feel about him." Allison absentmindedly withdrew her hand from Brendon's. She reached for the wine glass on the table and held it with both hands. "I was so caught up in my own grief that I didn't give it much thought. For a while I wanted him to suffer as much as I had, to feel my pain, my grief. To see what it had done to Josh."

"Did you read any of the papers, or police reports?"

"No, I just couldn't bring myself to read the reports. I wouldn't let Josh watch any TV. Surely they were wrong about Doug. We left Houston immediately after Doug and Maddy died." Allison got up from the table and paced the length of the table. "I still have a hard time believing Doug would do something like that. It made no sense. He wasn't that kind of guy. He worked hard and was a good father." Allison stopped pacing and looked directly at Brendon. "I lied to Josh about how his dad died."

"Why?"

"I didn't want him to be ashamed of Doug, or to hate anyone because of it. That's one of the reasons I've pushed it out of my mind. I realized thinking about it would drive me crazy. I couldn't live like that. I couldn't let hatred or grief consume me. I still had to live."

"I admire you for being so strong."

"I'm not really strong. I didn't have a choice. I had to go on for Josh's sake. It's something that I don't like to dwell on." Allison took a seat next to Brendon. "Tell me what happened to you. I'd actually like to hear it from a policeman's perspective."

"I nearly died when I was shot. Everything happened so fast. It was early morning, and the sun was blinding. I had so much on my mind and it didn't quite register what was happening. Maybe a couple of seconds transpired before I was shot. At the time, I didn't understand I had been shot. It was like someone had taken a red hot sledgehammer to my chest. I fell over on a rack of potato chips, and to this day the smell of chips brings back those memories. I remember thinking if I lived I'd never eat another chip as long as I lived."

"That's why you acted that way when Josh pushed chips in your face."

Brendon didn't answer. He took a deep breath, gathering the courage to continue. "I can still remember the look in the man's eyes as he was dying on the floor."

"I'm sorry."

"Don't be." Brendon ran his hands through his hair. "I was in a coma for two weeks, had several blood transfusions, and nearly died. After I got home from the hospital, Krishna–"

"Krishna?"

"He was the owner of the store where the shooting happened. He and his wife helped me for a while. Sometimes my buddies from the police force stopped by my apartment to help me. After a while, it was just me. I basically did nothing for two years except try to drink away my problems. I blamed myself for what happened."

"For getting shot?" Allison asked.

The silence and tension was as thick as the air was heavy. He wanted to tell her the rest of the story, and he knew he should before their relationship went any further. He couldn't hurt the woman he loved. It would destroy her, knowing he was the one who pulled the trigger, killing her husband. And now, he wasn't sure he could ever tell her. He could keep the secret, and in a small country town, far away from the big city, nobody knew his secret. Maybe that's the way it should be. Could he keep it from her? Forever? He thought it was worth a try.

"It's too difficult for me to talk about it anymore," Brendon said.

"Thank you for telling me," Allison said. "It means a lot to me."

Brendon nodded. "Would you like another glass of wine?"

"Yes."

After Brendon returned, they sat to the side sipping and drinking wine. A third cup later, Allison started feeling the effects.

They finished the wine, and Brendon guided Allison along to the other booths, where fresh green beans, squash, tomatoes, and strawberry and tomato preserves were available for sampling. She spread a little rosy-colored jam on a cracker, and giggling she popped the whole cracker in Brendon's mouth. He chewed and swallowed hard, making a face. "I think I'll be on a sugar high for the next year. What *was* that?"

"My favorite, tomato preserves."

"You put that in spaghetti sauce or something?" he asked, wiping his mouth with a napkin.

"No, silly. It's like jelly or jam."

"Oh, that explains why it's so sweet."

They strolled from booth to booth, sampling all sorts of high caloric deep fried Twinkies and Oreos, Snicker bars, and other things he never imagined that could be covered with a gooey coating and deep fried to a golden brown. Allison reminded him that *everything* could be deep fried. "It's the south, after all." From time to time, Josh came up to them asking his mother if he could have a few extra bucks. When she asked him what for, he mumbled saying he wanted to win a prize at the baseball tossing contest.

The band returned from their break; a few off key chords from an electric guitar broke the din of the crowd.

"Time to dance," she said to Brendon.

The announcer said, "Now, for all you grownup wild children of the seventies and eighties I'm going dedicate this next song to you. It's one of my favorites, or should I say my wife's favorites." He paused and looked at the sky. "God rest her soul. Come on out to the dance floor and get close, and be glad you have someone." He bowed his head, motioned to the piano player, who deftly keyed chords of the piano, then a run, followed by a soft violin crescendo. Taking the mike in his hands, the singer swayed to the beat of the song, mesmerized by the night air and of a memory a long time ago when he was young.

> *Hope they never end this song.*
> *This could take us all night long.*
> *I looked at the moon and I felt blue.*
> *Then I looked again and I saw you.*

"I don't think I've ever heard this song," Allison commented. "Have you?"

"Wait, I can't quite remember...yes...I know it," Brendon said tapping the air. "It's from the *Urban Cowboy* soundtrack."

A group of teenagers ran past them, muttering something about going down to the river where they couldn't be seen by the prying eyes of their parents. Someone flicked a half-smoked cigarette to the side. More couples moseyed toward the dance area. It was a dry, crunchy spot of grass that hadn't been watered in a month due to the water restrictions from the ongoing drought.

"Come on, this is one of the best love songs ever," Brendon said in Allison's ear. He guided her to the dance floor and pulled her close, resting a hand in the small of her back, their opposing hands loosely clasped.

They swayed together, fitting together perfectly as the songs segued into another.

Allison turned her head, resting her chin on his shoulder.

"I love you," Brendon whispered in her ear.

"I love you, too," Allison said.

For a few tantalizing moments they danced in silence, their bodies flush together, swaying in unison to the music, moonlight dancing upon them. Brendon took in the smell of her hair and ran his fingers though her long blonde locks.

The music slowed and they were so caught up in the moment they didn't realize the current song had ended.

Brendon guided Allison back over to where they were standing near the wine table and ordered them another glass of wine. They sipped wine together, laughing and talking, never running out of things to talk about. Allison tilted her head back, enjoying the moment.

Right then, Josh came running up, his friend Carter Smith right behind him. "Mom, can I spend the night with Carter? Please, please?" he asked impatiently. He took a bite out of the corn on the cob he was holding.

"I don't know." Allison turned to Brendon, needing confirmation, for what reason she wasn't sure, perhaps at the thought the night might allude to something else.

Without hesitating, Brendon gestured yes. "As long as it's okay with your mom."

"Thanks, Mom!" Josh exclaimed looking at his mom. "Next time I see Mrs. Harrigan I'll thank her for suggesting it."

"Oh, I see." Allison nodded slowly, the realization sinking in. "I think I know what's going on." She glanced at Brendon, who shrugged. Allison turned back to Carter. "Where is your mom?"

"She's over there, standing next to Mrs. Harrigan." Carter pointed to the other side of the dance floor. Allison glanced that way. Susan Harrigan had a smug look on her face.

"Mind your manners and be sure to say please and thank you!" Allison shouted as Josh and Carter ran off.

"Boys," she said, shaking her head. "I think they are conspiring against us."

"Maybe with us."

Allison smiled.

"You're doing a fabulous job raising him," Brendon said. "He's a great kid."

"Thank you," Allison said quietly. "He's getting to

that age where he really needs a father."

"Let's take a walk," Brendon suggested. He guided her away from the stage and the noise and bright lights of the county festival, away from the tents and double parked cars. They walked arm in arm toward Main Street where Allison's shop was located, then to the street beyond that until they came to the banks of the river.

They walked silently, enjoying the stroll, listening to nature's soundtrack: the river flowing, a squawking night hawk soaring above them, the quiet distant hum of the county fair.

They walked down a grassy embankment to a park that had been constructed on the banks of the river. A bustle of activity during the day, it was quiet and empty now. Away from the park Brendon spotted a grassy knoll, freshly cut, where he picked out a spot under a towering cypress tree, its branches laying low to the river. "Let's go over here."

Brendon sat down, resting against the trunk of the tree. Allison sat next to him and curled her legs sideways beneath her. She tucked her skirt under her legs. She extended her hand to the ground, the other one she rested in her lap.

In the moonless sky far removed from the lights of the city and the county fair, stars twinkled in the sky.

They sat in silence for a little while waiting for their eyes to adjust to the darkness.

A sad lullaby from the carnival played in the background among the soft chatter of customers sitting on the patio of the River Tavern. Water lapped against the pilings of the wooden pier.

"If you bend your head a little and look past the trees on the other side of the bank you can see the Big Dipper," Brendon said, pointing his hand to the sky.

"I'm impressed. You know your asterisms?"

"Aster, what?" he asked.

"I guess not." Allison said. "They are called as·ter·isms," she said, enunciating each syllable. "They are groups of stars in constellations. The Big Dipper is part of the Ursa Major constellation."

Brendon laughed. "I only know the Big Dipper because that's the only one we could ever see at night in Houston. Lights are too bright to see the stars clearly."

"Did you know you can always find north by finding the last star of the bowl of the big Dipper? Then, follow a straight line to the next star. That's Polaris. The North Star. It's the first star of the handle of the Little Dipper. See it?"

Brendon squinted in the darkness. "I think so." He moved his head closer to Allison, taking in the shape of her face highlighted against the dark sky, the curve of her chin, the way her lips moved when she talked.

Somewhere close by a fish jumped in the river sending ripples across the water. From the top of one of the sycamores, an owl hooted its loneliness.

"Have you been listening to me?"

"Yes, of course," Brendon said.

Testing him, Allison asked, "Did you know that the North Star is part of the Little Dipper?"

"No I didn't." Brendon broke off a blade of grass and tickled her arm with it. "Which one is the north star?" he asked, not really caring. He was much more interested in Allison and what the night had to bring.

"You haven't even been listening! That tickles. Stop it. You're distracting me," she laughed.

"That's the plan."

Allison tilted her head up toward the sky. "Seriously, Brendon, look to the stars."

"That's what Madison said to do."

"You remembered."

"I've remembered everything you've said."

"The North Star is in a straight line from the last star on the Big Dipper's bowl," Allison explained. "The seventh star."

He stopped tickling her and looked up to the sky. "I still don't see it." Brendon said. "If I'm ever stranded in the Sahara Desert, I'll look for the Little Dipper."

She playfully pushed him. "You never know when you might need to know the way north." Allison reached for his hand and lifted it to the sky. She held his hand and counted out loud each star. When she got to the last one she said, "Seventh and brightest one. It means good luck." She let go of his hand. "Now tell me again: which is the North Star?"

Brendon looked up at the sky and found the Big Dipper. He asked if the handle would always be facing up. Allison explained that it depended on the season of the year and since they were north of the equator, it would always be found either high or low in the northern sky. During spring and summer the Big and Little Dippers shined high in the sky. In autumn and winter, it was low in the sky. "Remember spring up, fall down." She stopped talking and gazed at the sky, taking in its dark beauty and unfathomable expanse. "If you make a wish, it will come true."

"Do we both make a wish?"

"Yes."

"At the same time?"

"Yes," she said, gazing into his eyes. "You have to close your eyes and make a wish," Allison said.

"You first."

Allison lowered herself down to the ground, the grass bending to the contours of her body. She stretched out and exhaled deeply.

Brendon looked at her and silently made a wish. She was absolutely beautiful. Blonde hair falling over her shoulders, skin like cream.

The tension between them was as thick and delicious as butter icing on a three-tiered vanilla cake.

They could both feel it.

They both wanted it.

They both wanted to taste it.

While Allison lay on the ground, she thought about how long it had been since she had been in the arms of a man she loved, one who returned her affection. It was right to be here with him. The evening had been perfect. The dance, darkness cocooning them in invisibility, the wine relaxing her, she couldn't have asked for a more perfect evening or timing. The two of them, close, stars overhead...

From the moment he walked into her store, she knew he was something special. It was like they didn't even need to speak to know one another, like old couples who sit quietly in a restaurant, communicating an entire life's worth of dreams and memories.

A hot breeze rustled the trees, leaves whispered lonely words, a few dark clouds floated among the stars, hiding their brightness.

She opened her eyes and looked into Brendon's soul, inviting him closer.

Understanding her non-verbal cue, Brendon shifted his weight and leaned over and kissed her on the mouth. She responded by putting her arm around his shoulders, gently pressing down, guiding him to her. He moved a leg on top of her, careful not to put his full body weight on her, and kissed her deeply, passionately.

They stayed like that for a long time, kissing and enjoying the pleasure of each other. Her lips parted as he ran his hand along her waist and pulled her closer, kissing her neck, her cheeks, tenderly, softly. She arched her back in subtle delight.

In the sky, stars twinkled, raining their magic dowr upon the night. Frogs croaked in the distance and w?

lapped against the lush banks of the Colorado River. In the night, nothing else mattered, only the two of them clothed in the darkness, safe from whatever private monsters lurked in their souls.

Far away tiny explosions filled the air, first one, then another and another, followed by high-pitched whistling noises until the sky flashed rhythmic starbursts of luminescent yellows and purples and blues.

"What was that?" Allison whispered.

"Fireworks," Brendon murmured. "It must be ten o'clock. The fair will close soon." He gave her a puzzled look then paused before saying, "Let's get crazy all alone."

She laughed quietly. "Isn't that a line from the song we danced to?"

"Ah, you remembered."

"What do you have in mind?" Allison propped herself up on her elbows.

"Let's go skinny dipping," Brendon said, arching an eyebrow, a hint of mischievousness in his voice.

"In the river?" Allison was incredulous. "Are you kidding! I'm not getting in there. You can't see two inches in front of you in that soup. There must be catfish the size of dolphins in there!"

"No, not the river. I wouldn't go in there either even in my life depended on it. I'm talking about a little spring-fed pool about half a mile from here, hidden downriver."

"How did you find it?"

"I came here with Bo a couple of weeks ago to take him walking. He ran off the trail chasing some animal. He wouldn't come when I called so I had to go get him, and that's when I found it. It's so close to the city, people are all around, and I couldn't believe there weren't a bunch of teenagers hanging around. It's very private. The best kept secret around here. Are you game?"

Allison pondered a short second before answering, "Yes I am."

He extended his hand, and she clasped her fingers around his hand. He helped her up, and they walked along the banks of the river, crawled over some brush, through a fence, stepped around trees, until finally they came to the spring.

Like a teenager doing something naughty, it was quite frankly exhilarating and terrifying at the same time to Allison.

Crickets cut the silence around them, and a falling star streaked across the sky, spreading a sparkle of light.

Clear, cool, spring-fed water bubbled gently up and through the pebbly bottom of the pool. Large glacial-scoured rocks lined the perimeter of the pool, spaced evenly like someone had placed them there. Mosses covered in yellow-green velvet blanketed the east side facing rocks. Green, spongy grass filled in the spaces among the rocks, and went up and around on the sloping knoll.

By now, their eyes had become accustomed to the darkness. Brendon ran his hands through his hair, and for the first time she noticed tawny streaks framing his face. His eyes looked darker, as well.

They fully gave in to the magic of July fourth, the distant fireworks, soft music, darkness, the two of them alone.

It was perfect.

Allison stood facing Brendon, her eyes misting over, and they stared at each other for a long few seconds. He cupped her face in his hands, bringing her closer. Her lips parted naturally, and his strong and sensual ones delivered what she expected. He kissed her softly at first, then stronger, and the longer he kissed her, the more ardent the moment became. She brought her arms up and to his back, running her hands along the curvature of his back, feeling his strength. He placed his hands on the small of her back and brought her closer, the two of them in the night, alone, caught up in the moment.

He released her and she stepped back. She removed her sandals, feeling the cool grass upon her feet. Allison felt as though she was in a dream, still warm from the wine, warm from the July heat.

The moment was heady.

In the silence Allison undid the belt around her waist, letting it fall to the ground. Brendon helped her slip off her white blouse, up and over her head. He kissed her again, on the tip of her nose, the eyelids, cheeks, and neck, kissing more as he moved along her bare skin, exploring her body. She shuddered with delight.

He stood back and undid each button on his shirt until finally the last one came undone. He draped the shirt over one of the rocks.

Together, they removed their remaining clothes until they stood barefoot and naked under the sky and the stars.

Their skin became supple in the heat.

Hot wouldn't aptly describe the heat. It was all around them, like sitting in a steamy sauna after a hard workout.

The natural seventy-two degrees pool beckoned them with refreshing water, clearer than the best maintained swimming pool.

Brendon slipped into the cool water, barely making a ripple. Goose pimples appeared all over his arms until his body acclimated to the water. He slid further into the pool, stretching his toes, reaching for the bottom. At its deepest, the water came to the top of his chest.

He reached for Allison's hand, guiding her toward

him. Bending at the knees, Allison held his hand and lowered herself into the cool water, one leg at a time. He brought her to him, twirling her, splashing water over the rocks. They laughed quietly at the pebbles and water grass ticking their toes, laughed at the hot breeze rustling the trees.

Together they submerged, the water blanketing them in a soundless universe where only they existed. There were no outside influences or societal constraints to worry about, inhibiting them, only their bodies pressed together.

It was titillating.

He kissed her underwater and moved his hands over her shoulders and back. He took his time, exploring her body without rushing or making demands on her.

Never once did she pull back or hesitate.

Allison went to the surface first, tilting her head back, her skin glistening in the reflection of the stars upon the water. Using both hands she smoothed her hair away from her face as she treaded water. Brendon came up for a breath too, blowing little bubbles on the water's surface.

She gave him a playful splash.

He shook the water from his face, and gliding through the water, he reached over, taking her by her waist until they came together. He propped her up on his knee, and using the buoyancy of the water, he took her to the place they both wanted to be.

Chapter 20

Lee checked his watch. Eleven pm.

"Shit," he muttered, stumbling along the fairgrounds, cheap booze sloshing out of the cup he held. *Where was she*? Lee came up to an empty beer can, mumbled something about litterers then kicked the beer can as hard as he could. The crowd had thinned out, the musicians had all left, and a few snotty-nosed kids ran amuck, leaving Lee alone with his thoughts and a throbbing head.

Allison's car was still parked in the same spot, so he knew she was still here. He desperately wanted to apologize for his behavior the other night, but every time there was an opportunity to talk to Allison, Mr. Hotshot made his presence known, like he was some kind of male lion challenging Lee over territory.

Lee's territory.

He had been in this Godforsaken town for nearly twenty years, and if it hadn't been for his wife and that slick lawyer of hers, Lee would be sitting poolside at a resort somewhere having cabana boys wait on him. Make that a cabana *girl*, because after all, he wouldn't want to give the wrong impression.

Dammit to hell. He was stuck. He had blown through almost all of the life insurance money making bad investments and he couldn't sell the land because his wife had made some sort of fancy will stipulating only their sons could sell the land. Lee could live in the house and use the land as long as he wanted to, but he could never sell it. *Bitch*, he thought.

Sitting down at a picnic table, he stretched and rested his back on the table.

He took the flask he kept hidden under his shirt, poured a shot, then swallowed hard, feeling the burn of the whiskey. He wiped his mouth using the back of his hand. Thinking about Brendon and Allison getting all touchy-feely made him want to puke. When he thought about them together, enough rage boiled up inside of him to blow off the top of Mount St. Helens. He banged a balled fist on the wooden table.

He really thought he could kill someone about now.

Lee swallowed the last of the whiskey and tossed the cup. The janitor or cleaning crew could pick it up. They got paid, so what was the big deal?

"Hey, Lee," a voice called out. It was Harbin Schuler, the editor of the local newspaper.

"Harbin," Lee said, giving him a sup nod. "What are you doing out here so late? Don't you have to go write copy or something?"

"Nah." Harbin came over to where Lee sat, propped one foot on the bench, took a toothpick from his shirt pocket, and started cleaning his teeth. "I got some interns from the journalism department at the local community college doing all the late night work. Don't even pay them. They're too stupid to ask for compensation." He elbowed Lee then snickered. "Know what I mean?"

"Yeah," Lee said, laughing thinly.

"What are you doing here by yourself?" Harbin asked. "I thought you mentioned you had some big plans with Allison."

"I blew her off."

"Hmm." Harbin mulled Lee's comment over before he continued. "You know I have a good view of her shop from my office window. All I have to do is swivel my chair and look through those big store windows."

"So? What's your point?"

"If you don't move in on her, I will."

"You're not her type."

Harbin dug around between his teeth, and when he found a goody, he wiped the toothpick on his trousers. "I know who is."

Lee grunted. "Let me guess." He hocked a mouthful of spit into the grass. "You haven't seen her by any chance, have you?"

"Actually, I have. She left about an hour ago with that new guy in town." Harbin flicked the toothpick away.

"Shit!" Lee glared at Harbin. "Where'd they go?"

"Saw them walking toward the river."

"Why didn't you tell me?" Lee demanded.

"Hey," Harbin exclaimed, putting his hands up. "Don't shoot the messenger. I thought you said you blew her off."

"More like the other way around. If it wasn't for that new guy in town–"

"That McMahon guy."

"You know him?" Lee asked.

"Never been formally introduced," Harbin said, shifting his weight to the other foot. "Wait till you hear what I found out."

"Something good?"

"Better than good."

Harbin reached into his shirt pocket for another toothpick. "About a month ago, I can't exactly remember when it was, but it was a slow news day. Anyway, I was sitting at my desk watching the tourists on Main Street when you walked into her store. I watched y'all for a

162

while. Caught you looking down her shirt."

"You lecherous voyeur," Lee snickered.

"Like I said, it was a slow news day. I noticed some guy in a truck parked outside of Allison's shop. At the time I didn't recognize him and I didn't think much of it until he peeled out of there, then wouldn't you know it? He came right back. I thought it was kinda odd, maybe he was casing the place, so I wrote down his license plate."

"Did you run his plates?" Lee asked.

"Nah. I got busy and forgot about it until I saw them together tonight."

"What's the big deal? I don't care if he sits outside of her shop."

"Being the judicious reporter that I am..."

Lee huffed.

"...my curiosity got the best of me so I hightailed it back to my office, dug around in my desk until I found the Post-it with the plate number. Fortunately for you I never threw it away. My buddy at the sheriff's just got back to me after running his plates."

"What d'ya find out?"

"It's a doozy of a story," Harbin said. He was salivating at the mouth like a starving dog devouring a bone.

"Well don't let grass grow under your feet, you son-of-a-bitch. Tell me!"

Harbin leaned in close to Lee. "Get this: he had been on the Houston police force for ten years when he was involved in a shooting." He paused for emphasis. "He killed a guy."

"So?" Lee shrugged. "Probably some drug dealer. He did the world a favor."

"He wasn't a drug dealer. He was a family guy, *and* wait till you hear this." For emphasis, Harbin lowered his voice, speaking slowly. "His name was Doug

Hartley."

It took a moment for Lee to digest what Harbin had told him, and when he did his eyes got about as big around as a full moon. He shot off of the bench. "Doug Hartley?" he repeated.

"Yeah, and you know who Doug Hartley is, don't you?" Harbin asked.

"Allison's dead husband."

Chapter 21

Later that night, they put their clothes on, found their cars where they had left them, and drove back to Allison's house. Feeling protective of her, Brendon followed Allison home, wanting to make sure nothing happened. When they got to her house, she asked him to park his car behind the garage so prying eyes and wagging tongues driving on the county road wouldn't have fodder for the next day's gossip.

He rolled his car to a stop and cut the headlights and engine. In the total darkness they walked hand in hand to the front steps of Allison's house. Something scurried and rustled the dry grass and pine needles bunched up against the house. "Probably a raccoon or possum," Brendon said.

They laughed and giggled, acting like teenagers as they walked up the stairs of her front porch.

Content she was safe, Allison unlocked the front door and stepped in, Brendon right behind her. When she shut the front door, he scooped her up, holding her like a groom about to carry his bride over the threshold.

Allison threw her arms around his neck, resting her head on his shoulder. "I think I could get used to this."

"We're alone right?" Brendon asked.

"Yes. Josh won't be home until ten in the morning."

"Which is your room?"

"The one down the hall and to the left."

He carried her and she laughed when her foot bumped into the wall. He walked to her bedroom, pushed open the door with his foot, and set her gently down on the bed. They both undressed and slipped into the neatly made bed with two fluffy pillows, cotton sheets, and a sea-green duvet cover, welcoming the fresh sheets next to their bare skin.

The air-conditioner window unit blew cool air, the sheer curtains blowing in the man-made breeze.

Wrapped in each other's arms, Allison fell asleep resting her head next to his chest.

Brendon didn't fall asleep. He lay awake thinking about his life.

If they were to have a future together, he would have to come clean about his past. When? How to tell her? Tonight wasn't the right time. This was the first time in years he had really been alive, unencumbered by the pressures and dangerous work a man in blue faces every day.

After the shock of the shooting had worn off, he had come to realize that working as a policeman had become unbearable, and the stress had started to manifest in physical symptoms. He could never go back to that work.

He became more at ease wearing faded blue jeans and a T-shirt instead of a constricting uniform, although he missed the camaraderie of his fellow police officers. Working outside on the house and land provided ample time for him to reflect on his life. Leading an active life, he had become leaner, building muscle by hauling fence posts, hammering nails, not to mention the leg workout he got climbing ladders to paint the house. No amount of time with a hundred dollar an hour trainer in an air-conditioned gym would compensate for the real thing. No machine could duplicate the action of swinging an ax.

Wide awake, Brendon stared at the faded bead board

ceiling, long two-inch planks of wood, painted a pastel blue that ran parallel to the hallway. It was similar to the ceiling in his ranch house. In fact, a lot of things about this house were similar to his. The angle of the ceilings, the same doorknobs, even the windows with their warped glass.

Ambient moonlight filtered in through the sheer curtains. Her bedroom was cozy and inviting, almost like a bed and breakfast inn city people paid lots of money for to enjoy a weekend retreat. Opposite the bed, on an old chest-of-drawers, several pictures were displayed.

Mindful not to wake Allison, he slid out of bed and went over to the dresser to inspect the carefully placed family pictures. In one of them, Allison was holding Madison, who appeared to be about three, with Doug standing next to her. Josh was leaning into his dad. A searing pang of regret tugged at Brendon. So that's what her husband looked like alive. Doug was smiling, practically unrecognizable from the image seared into his mind, and definitely not the same desperate man he had shot.

Setting the picture down, he noticed a few books stacked neatly and he looked at those, several being by well-known authors. Since they weren't in the genre he liked, he didn't peruse any.

He tiptoed back to the bed, the floorboards creaking under his feet, and quietly slid into bed, careful not to disturb Allison. For a while, and he wasn't quite sure how long it was, he lay there. From time to time, he would brush loose stands of hair away from Allison's face.

He could definitely get used to this.

While Allison slept, he was fully aware of how satisfied he felt, that she was the one for him.

Though the air-conditioner window unit placed in the outside wall of the bedroom ran at full speed, the heat marched into the room. The air-conditioner kept up a valiant fight against the heat, forcing it to retreat before pushing onwards again. It went on for hours. He pushed down the covers to his waist, letting the air-conditioned air cool his chest. He clasped his hands behind his head and looked at the digital clock on the bedside stand. It was almost 4 am. He had been awake since they had gotten back to her place, and he really didn't want to sleep.

He didn't want this night to ever end.

Outside, the moon crept across the sky, illuminating the pines in soft light. The land was dry, the air hot, and Brendon finally fell asleep looking at the one he loved.

Sunlight streamed in though the sheer curtains, bathing the room in a warm glow. Allison rubbed her eyes, yawning.

She couldn't remember the last time she had slept so soundly. There was something comforting sleeping next to the one you love: the warmth of the bed, connection to another human being, soft breathing. They had only known each other a short time, and it was totally out of character for her to do what she did last night.

Yet, at the same time it was right.

She did love Brendon.

Stretching her feet to the end of the bed, she listened to the comforting noises of her home: the humming air-conditioner unit, the mockingbirds haggling over feeding space under the oak tree, a white-winged dove cooing in the tree tops, a branch scraping against the roof.

Something wasn't right.

She threw the covers off the bed and swung her feet over the side. Where *was* Brendon?

She glanced at the clock. It was almost ten. Would Josh come home and find Brendon here? Had Brendon left without saying goodbye? Did he think she did that all the time? A thousand thoughts bounced around her mind like marbles on a tin roof and the cacophony in her head made no sense.

One thing was for sure: Josh would be home soon.

Allison threw on a T-shirt and some jeans, bolted to the den, hoping Brendon would be making scrambled eggs and toast, offering her a cup of coffee. Her shoulders dropped when she realized that would not have been possible because she had not gone grocery shopping. The refrigerator and pantry were almost empty.

She went to the window and checked behind the garage where he had parked his truck, only to see the tire impressions in the grass where his truck had been parked.

Her heart sank.

She couldn't believe after the night they had spent together, and how they had professed their love for one another he would leave. Could she have been wrong about him? Was she making it up? All the things he had whispered in her ear while they were dancing, while they were alone together skinny dipping, making love.

A car rolling into the driveway got her attention. She checked herself in a mirror, fluffed her hair, and wiped the smeared mascara from under her eyes. Good enough. She took a deep breath, steadying herself. She went to the front door opened it hoping to see Brendon. Instead, Josh bounded up the front porch stairs followed by a blast of hot air.

"Hi, Mom," he said, bolting into the house.

"Nice to see you too."

Allison walked down the stairs and went over to the car, standing near the driver's side.

Carter's mother, Brenda, rolled down the window and peered up at Allison. "The boys had a really good time. And Josh had breakfast. He's probably good until lunch," she said. "You know how these boys can eat when they have a growth spurt!" She gave Allison a puzzled look. "You okay? You look like you just got up."

"Oh, yes. I slept in. It's been a long time since I slept this late. "Guess I didn't know how tired I was."

"I meant to ask you, who was that guy you were dancing with last night?"

Allison shrugged, pretending to look at something in the countryside. "One of my customers."

"Didn't know sewing was so exciting."

"I can tell you it's not. Thanks so much for letting Josh spend the night, and for bringing him back," Allison said. She was reluctant to continue the conversation.

"Anytime. Gotta run. See you later," Brenda said.

Allison waved goodbye while Brenda backed out of the driveway. After her car disappeared from sight, Allison turned around to go inside when something stopped her. She paused, listening to the hum of a vehicle approaching on the road.

The truck came into view and Allison immediately recognized it as Brendon's. She smiled the biggest, happiest smile.

Brendon parked the truck and got out, carrying two bags of groceries filled with eggs and bacon, fresh cantaloupe and strawberries, biscuit mix, and milk. He had even gotten cream for coffee. Bo came bounding out of the truck.

"I thought you had left. I was worried," Allison said.

"About what?" Brendon commented.

"I...I don't know."

Anxiety stretched across her face, and he understood. Brendon put down the groceries.

"Come here. Look at me, please." He put his hands on her shoulders. "Last night was magical. Allison, I love you, and I realized I loved you from the first time I saw

170

you. I never believed in love at first sight until I met you. Now I understand. I got up early because I wanted to make you a country breakfast with all the trimmings so I could surprise you with breakfast in bed," he said. "There wasn't anything in the fridge. You were sleeping soundly so I didn't want to disturb you." He paused then continued, "I'm sorry. I thought I'd be back before you got up. I also had to let Bo out of the house. He'd been in there since I left yesterday."

Allison nodded. She placed her index finger to her lips. "Josh is home. I don't want him to hear us."

"Oh," Brendon's eyes darted to the house. "Do you want me to leave?"

"No, make something up."

"Like what?"

"Say that you saw me outside and stopped to say hello. And, and..." Allison was thinking fast now, "and that I invited you in to make breakfast."

"Think Josh will believe that?" Brendon asked.

"He'd better."

Bo wandered up the driveway, stopped when he reached the porch, sniffed something, and lifted his leg before trotting up the stairs. He pawed at the screen door waiting to be let in.

"Makes himself right at home, doesn't he?" Allison commented.

Allison invited Brendon in, and together they gave their made-up, feeble explanation to Josh. He seemed satisfied, and fortunately didn't ask any questions. Allison sensed he was more interested in playing with Bo.

"Josh has always wanted a dog," Allison said wistfully.

"Why don't you get him one?" Brendon asked.

"I'm not home much, and between work and shuttling

Josh around, there isn't much home time. Besides, when we are here, I'm either helping Josh with homework or taking care of the place."

"Allison, it *is* the country. All you need is a fenced in yard. Boys and dogs go together like peas and carrots."

"I don't like peas and carrots."

"Me neither," Brendon said. "It was the only expression I could think of!"

"Speaking of the fenced in yard, are you volunteering your services?" Allison asked with a twinkle in her voice.

"It'll cost you."

"You're going to charge me?"

"Not really. Maybe we can make a trade?"

"I'm sure I can think of something," she said with a wink.

Brendon made Allison the breakfast he said he would, waiting on her hand and foot, only letting her tell him where to find the skillet and utensils he needed. She really fought the urge to help him or instruct him the best way to scramble eggs and how much the heat should be set to, deciding to let him make the breakfast any way he wanted to. Regardless of how it turned out, having someone else cook for her was a luxury Allison had not experienced in a long while. However Brendon cooked breakfast, she would lavish praise on him.

Allison sat at the kitchen table while Brendon busied himself in the kitchen. He was making a mess, dirtying almost every single dish and bowl she had. He spilled flour from the biscuit mix all over the counter. Coffee grinds ended up on the floor. He dropped an egg, which landed with a sickening splat on the floor garnering Bo's attention. Rising from his curled position, ears cocked, his nostrils twitched at the hint of food, and he trotted over to the kitchen, tail wagging. He looked at his owner, waiting for instruction.

"Do what you do best, Bo," Brendon instructed. Bo lapped up the broken egg, careful to lick around the shell. "He's my built-in mop," Brendon explained.

Allison cleared her throat, twice, to get Brendon's attention. She tapped her nose then wiggled her finger at Brendon.

He got the message. Taking a paper towel, he dotted his nose to remove the smudge of flour.

He insisted on frying bacon instead of microwaving it, heeding what Allison had said. After he fried the bacon, he emptied the drippings into the trash can, leaving a little to cook the scrambled eggs with, and to give them added flavor.

"What are you smiling about? Hopefully not at my pathetic cooking skills," he said raising an eyebrow.

"No, *no*, of course not." She paused a few moments while she looked at him. Her eyes twinkled. "This might take us all morning long."

"What?"

She willed him with her eyes.

"Oh...right," he said understanding the slightly different song lyrics. "I'd like to spend it all with you."

Brendon played the part magnificently, mixing up some of the lyrics from the song from last night, interspersing them into his conversation. Things like, *"You wouldn't lie to me,"* or *"Close your eyes,"* and *"After all is said and done."* She'd smile and try to think of lines from the song to answer him back, all the while, thinking Josh was oblivious to the word's secret meanings.

During their clandestine conversation, Allison and Brendon failed to notice Josh had turned down the TV volume, and had, in fact, been listening intently to their conversation.

Propping himself up on his elbows from his position on the floor, Josh turned over to look at his mother and

Brendon.

"Are you guys talking in code or something?"

Brendon stopped stirring the scrambled eggs. He shot a *we've been caught* look at Allison.

"What?" Allison asked.

"Y'all are making no sense. I've been listening." Josh scowled at his mother.

"Grown up talk," she admonished. Allison took a big swallow of coffee. She looked down at the mug. "You've been watching too much TV. Turn it off and take Bo outside. He probably has to do his business."

"Okay," Josh huffed. "Come on, Bo."

When the screen door slammed shut and Josh was out of sight, Brendon went over to Allison and helped her up out of her chair. He took her by the waist, bringing her close, and kissed her fully on her lips. They stayed like that for a while, hugging and kissing, and when Brendon abruptly pulled away, it was because a pattering of footsteps on the porch announced the entrance of Josh and Bo.

"I saw that. Y'all are gross."

Allison smiled and took a seat at the kitchen table, sipping coffee, enjoying the moment. She had forgotten what it was like to have another adult in the house, someone she could have a meaningful conversation with. Things of their generation they could laugh about, songs they remembered from the 90s, bad fashions, and laughing about old technology.

"Breakfast is ready," Brendon announced.

"Can I eat too?" Josh asked.

"I thought you already had breakfast," Allison said.

"Yeah, but I'm hungry again."

They sat down at the table to a spread of steamy scrambled eggs still in the cast iron skillet, a basket of homemade biscuits covered with a checkered cloth napkin, fresh butter, cubed cantaloupe, sliced strawberries, and a pound of bacon. Nestled between Brendon and Josh, Bo patiently waited for a morsel to be thrown his way.

When Josh didn't think his mother was looking, he'd sneak a tidbit of bacon to Bo.

After eating, Brendon and Josh cleared the table and soaked the dishes, forbidding Allison to do any work. Afterwards, Brendon suggested he and Allison go sit on the back porch to polish off the last of the coffee.

Brendon held the screen door open, motioning for Allison to go first. Bo and Josh stayed inside, Josh watching TV and petting Bo.

"That, I believe, was the best breakfast I've ever had," Allison admitted, exhaling a satisfied breath.

"It's one of my hidden talents," Brendon said.

Allison walked over to one of the chairs, sat down, and took a sip of coffee. She had changed into a pair of shorts and a tangerine colored T-shirt, the color complimenting her summer tan. No make-up though, she didn't need it. Her skin was radiating the way she felt.

Brendon joined her and they talked the rest of the morning away, Allison giggling like a school girl at times, much to his pleasure. Sometimes they sat in silence gazing upon the countryside.

It was July 5th, noontime, too hot for most animals to be active, except for the lonely singing of a mockingbird, or the flight of a field sparrow. At times cicadas chirped in the sweltering heat, first one then another until the symphony hit a crescendo before falling silent.

A hot breeze rustled the pine trees behind Allison's house, and crunchy pine needles fell to the forest floor like a hot prickly rain.

Chapter 22

Hot damn! If Lee held his newfound knowledge any longer, he might burst. His nervous energy was palpable even though he had finished a five mile jog on the county road. It just so happened that his jogging route took him by Allison's house, and wouldn't you know it? Mr. Hotshot's truck was parked in front of the house.

Lee smirked.

Let Brendon enjoy it while it lasted, which wouldn't be much longer.

Arriving back home, Lee slung the front door open, went over to the fridge, and opened a cold bottle of water.

It couldn't get any better than this. Lee knew the whole time Brendon had been holding back something. From the first time they met, the guy had copped an attitude, and for what reason? Lee had tried to be neighborly, stopping by Brendon's house, introducing himself. Not to mention a good-looking bachelor like Brendon didn't show up out of the wild blue Texas yonder feigning interest in remodeling his parents' old house.

Not in a one-horse town like Bastrop.

Being the cunning man that he was, Lee knew something was up. Yeah, wait until he told Allison about Brendon.

It was Sunday afternoon, and Lee had been formulating his plan for hours. He thought about heading over to Allison's to tell her, doubting she would let him in, considering his drunken behavior the other day. That was stupid of him. However, he had wormed his way out of even more egregious behavior than that, so if he talked smoothly and brought her a present, she'd forgive him.

This morning, Lee had seen someone place a new vase of flowers at the cemetery which gave him an idea. He could swipe those before they wilted, put fresh water in the vase, stick everything in the fridge, and voila! He had the present. He mentally patted himself on the back for being so clever and thrifty, considering he found a way to repurpose the flowers before their usefulness ended. And wasn't that what all the *going green* shit was about? Recycling, repurposing, reutilize, and la-de-da-de-da... Who gave a flying flip? Lee didn't. He did need to keep up appearances with the younger Millennial generation though, so he did his duty when called upon.

Lee downed the last sip from the water bottle and tossed it in the trash. What difference would one bottle make?

Perhaps he needed a little more ammunition when he told Allison. He thought about how he could dig up dirt on Brendon because she might not take his word for it. The newspaper office was closed on Sundays so that wouldn't help.

Hmm.

Lee checked the time. The library should still be open and if he ran into town, he'd have just enough time to use the computers. A quick Google search should do the trick.

Game time.

Chapter 23

Over the next few days Brendon found excuses to come over to Allison's house after she got home from work. On Tuesday, he brought a new box of checkers for Josh, and he and Josh spent an hour playing in the den while Allison made dinner for all of them. Josh proved to be a formidable checkers player, and the only time Brendon won was when Josh became distracted by Bo.

On Wednesday Brendon brought over a length of sturdy rope and an old tire he picked up for a buck at the junk yard. "It's for a tree swing," he explained, looking up at a misshapen oak tree, gauging the branch best to hang the swing from.

"How are you going to climb up there?" Allison asked.

Brendon pondered the situation, scratching his chin and mulling over how he would do exactly that. Putting down the rope and tire, he turned around and left without an explanation, and when he came back, he had several two by fours, a hammer and nails. Placing the boards on the tree, he nailed them in and tested their sturdiness suitable for withstanding his full weight of 180 pounds.

"Good job," Allison told him, admiring how his muscles rippled under his shirt.

Brendon shimmied up the oak tree, hugged it tightly, and looped the rope around a high branch on the tree.

"You climb like a monkey!" Allison teased him.

Brendon replied back making jungle noises.

"I think you mean 'ah, ah, ting, tang, walla, walla, bing, bang," Allison sang.

"Good enough," Brendon called from the tree. He knotted the rope, pulling on it to test the strength of it. Satisfied, he climbed down and tied the tire to the rope then told Josh to try out the new swing.

Josh climbed into the tire. Holding onto the rope he pushed back with his feet and let go. He flew through the air and twisted and turned, laughing. Bo stood to the side, barking and running alongside of Josh, snapping playfully at his tennis shoes.

"Whew, it's hot!" Allison exclaimed. "I'll go make some lemonade."

Allison walked into the house and stood at the kitchen sink, squeezing the lemons into a pitcher. She looked out the window, watching Brendon push Josh higher and higher. "Not too high!" she yelled from the door. As she thought about Brendon, the way he laughed, how he held the door open for her, how they had made love for the second time, she knew he was the one for her.

On Friday evening Brendon paced the floor in his house, waiting for Allison to show up for their date. He wondered when he should tell her the real reason he came to Bastrop.

Sure, the house he inherited was a good excuse, it didn't raise any eyebrows, and she was satisfied with the reason, yet that little voice in his head screamed loud and clear that he should tell her. That gut feeling, lingering from his police days, spoke to him like a megaphone in his head.

He should tell her. Yet he couldn't force the words from his mouth because the more he thought about her, the more he loved her.

He admired her openness and willingness to move ahead with her life with what would have knocked most people to the floor. She was a strong woman, much stronger than most people he knew, and he couldn't imagine the fortitude it required for her to forge ahead after the death of her husband and daughter. It would have sent most people to the loony bin, and even though Brendon hadn't lost anyone the way Allison had, he had come close to being locked up in a padded cell.

He thought about what Krishna had said, "When the right time comes, you will find the words." Easier said than done. The right words kept him up at night, and he rehearsed the scene over and over. He couldn't bear hurting her, not after they had declared their love for each other.

Not after Josh had accidentally called him 'Dad' the other day.

Josh and Brendon were washing Allison's car, which was covered in a month's worth of dust. They had playfully splashed each other with the hose, taking turns horsing around until they were soaked from head to toe. After towel-drying the exterior and vacuuming the interior, Brendon had asked Josh to get him a fresh towel so he could dry off. Josh replied, "Sure, Dad."

Brendon almost corrected him, but watching Josh run into the house yelling for Allison to get a towel, he realized Josh *was* like a son to him, and he felt an overwhelming need to protect him. It was a profound bonding moment and it reminded Brendon of when he helped his own father while they worked on cars or did minor repairs.

He already had a built-in family, and he didn't plan on changing any of that with a confession.

Right on time, and with evening approaching,

Brendon saw the headlights of a car come into view along the country road. When the car turned into the driveway, he knew it was Allison, and he stepped out onto the porch to wait for her. In the dimming light, she was absolutely stunning. Her tight jeans accentuated her long legs, and her white blouse, tucked into belted jeans, flowed nicely to her hips. The belt buckle rounded out her country dancing ensemble.

When her eyes met Brendon's, she smiled an inviting smile.

Bo bounded off the steps and wiggled over to her. "Come here, Bo," Allison said. She bent down and playfully grabbed handfuls of fur along his neck, giving him a vigorous rub. Bo whined and wiggled, leaning into her.

"He's acting like he hasn't seen you in a week," Brendon said.

"He must have a short memory."

"Either that or he's hoping you have a treat for him."

"Ohh, Bo, so sorry," she said in baby-talk. "I don't have anything for you."

"He'll get over it." Brendon walked down the steps. "You look beautiful."

"You don't look so shabby either," she said, eyeing him over. "Are those new Wranglers?"

"Actually yes. I thought I'd look presentable for our first official date."

"You definitely pass the test."

"Ready to go dancing?"

"I am. Aren't you going to invite me in? I haven't even seen your place yet."

"Sure, come on in." Brendon held the door open for Allison to walk in, instructing Bo to come back inside. "If Bo is outside when it gets dark, he'll be gone for days."

"Doing what?"

"Chasing a raccoon."

"Why? It's not like you don't feed him," she said. "No offense Bo, but you're a well-fed dog."

Bo thumped his tail.

"It's the thrill of the hunt he's after. I don't exactly lead an exciting life, and Bo's not exactly a good helper. He sleeps on the job a lot."

Allison laughed.

"Besides, it's in his genes. Being part hound dog he can't help himself."

Brendon shut the door and Allison stood in the entryway.

She took a pensive look at the interior, checking the floors and ceilings. "I've driven by this place a hundred times. I was always in such a rush that I never took the time to really look at the house. You've done a lot of work, haven't you? It's clean too. I'm impressed."

Brendon had purposely tidied up the place in anticipation of her coming over. He had swept and dusted the few pieces of furniture, arranging a few books on the coffee tables because he knew she liked books. He swept the floor with the new Swiffer he had bought earlier in the week, dumbfounded by the amount of dog hair in the house, an observation he planned to keep to himself.

"I *have* done a lot," Brendon said proudly. "Come into the kitchen and let me show you. Want a beer?"

"I would," Allison said. A book on the coffee table piqued her interest. She picked it up, thumbing the pages. "A western, huh? I didn't know you liked to read."

"I do."

"What other secrets do you have?" Allison asked. Her voice was playful and she put the book down and came over to him, wrapping her arms around him.

He thought about saying *You don't know the half of it*, but he kept quiet and pulled her closer, putting a hand in the small of her back, gazing at her beauty and the way her hair fell to her shoulders. He kissed her on the lips, and she responded with an equally passionate kiss.

When Brendon pulled back, he said, "Hold that thought, okay?"

"Absolutely."

"How about that beer now?"

"What do you have?"

Opening the fridge he said, "I have an international selection of Dos Equis, Dos Equis, or Dos Equis."

"Hmm, that's a tough decision," Allison said. "I'll take the third option."

"Good choice." Brendon popped the top off, handed her the beer, and motioned for her to take a seat on the sofa. Allison sat down and crossed her legs.

"So," Allison said, "tell me what you've done with the house."

Brendon took a seat next to Allison. "When I first moved in this place was a mess. I even found a rat's nest in one of the cupboards."

Allison grimaced.

"The first to go was the vintage 70s shag carpet."

"Excellent decision," she said.

"Luckily the hardwoods were in decent shape, only needing a sanding and a new finish."

Allison tapped the floor with her boot. "Sounds solid."

"I've painted every room, cabinets too, and scrubbed about a century's worth of grime from the kitchen floor."

"You could have hired someone to do all that," Allison suggested.

"I know, but the work was cathartic for me."

Allison didn't comment right away. Her thoughts went to the time she had been doing her own housework prior to when Madison died, remembering how the domesticity had kept her sane. "Believe me, I understand that. For women I can understand. I thought men needed something more manly, like boxing or chopping down a tree. Why was housework cathartic for you?" Allison asked, her voice a mixture of motherly concern and genuine caring.

"I think I've been trying to scrub away the issues from my past. It's like what I did with the kitchen floor. I thought about covering up the tile with something inexpensive but that wouldn't solve the underlying problem, would it? It would be a cosmetic fix, like plastic surgery for someone trying to cover up their insecurities. Scrubbing the floor was hard and sweaty work and when I finally finished, I felt good about what I had done. Being here in the house made me face my past."

"The reasons for your nightmares, right?"

Brendon nodded. "Look down the hallway," he instructed with a motion of his head. "See how it's boarded up?"

Allison peered down the hallway. "I noticed it when I came in, but I didn't want to say anything. Is that part of what you're trying to deal with?"

Brendon took a long pull of beer and swallowed audibly. "That's the part of the house where the fire took place."

Allison set the beer down on a coaster, and leaned into him. "Tell me about it."

Brendon ran his index finger over the rim of his beer bottle. It was like he was in a trance, thinking about the tragedy so long ago when he was a child. He had known this time would come, when he had to talk about it, for keeping it bottled up inside was the reason for his nightmares.

Taking a deep breath, Brendon began. "My parents were celebrating their thirteenth wedding anniversary and had made reservations for a dinner in Austin. It was getting late and we were all sitting around waiting for the babysitter to show up. My mom was getting really antsy then the phone rang. It was the babysitter calling to cancel. They never went out to eat, so this was a big deal to them. My mom was so disappointed, so I told her that I could babysit Julie. I was only ten though. I told my mom I was mature for my age so I could take care of Julie and make sure she went to bed on time. My parents were a little apprehensive about leaving us here, but I assured them nothing would happen."

Brendon picked up the beer, twirled it, and took another long pull, letting out a heavy breath he had been holding.

"This is hard."

Allison put her hand on his knee. "I know."

"My mom gave me all sorts of instructions: keep the door locked, don't try to cook anything, don't let Julie stay up too late, don't go outside. All sorts of things. I told her not to worry because we would be fine. Julie begged my mom not to go, and kept crying even after they left. I told her she was a crybaby, which made her cry even more, and she wasn't interested when I tried to play Chutes and Ladders with her, so we watched TV. For a while Julie was okay until it was time to go to bed and then she started crying again. When she wouldn't stop, I told her she could sleep in Mom and Dad's bed, and that seemed to make her feel better."

Brendon kneaded his forehead, searching for the right words, trying to keep his composure. "If I hadn't let her sleep in there, she'd still be alive."

Allison heard the crack in his voice. She looked directly into his eyes. "I'm listening."

"I gave her a piggyback ride to my parent's bed," Brendon said. He paused before giving Allison a bleak smile. "I tucked her in and told her Mom and Dad would be back before she knew it. I even read her a bedtime story. I told her if she went to sleep, they'd get home quicker."

"Did it work?" Allison asked.

"Yes. She fell fast asleep." Brendon took another swallow of beer.

"What about you? What did you do?"

"I watched TV for a little while longer then fell asleep on the sofa. I'm not sure how long I had been asleep, but for some reason I woke up. It was hazy in the den and there was a strange crackling sound and an odd odor. I thought maybe my parents had come back and my mom had burned something in the oven. I didn't give it a second thought until Julie started screaming."

Brendon hung his head. "God, this is more difficult than I thought it would be." He cast a look at Allison and saw the concern in her eyes. "I've never talked about this to anyone."

Allison touched his arm with a warm hand, and he clasped it in his.

"It all happened so fast. I mean, the fire. It was like it wasn't there one second then the next second flames started shooting out from the bedroom. It was awful. Julie screamed these horrible screams...I can't get those out of my mind. I didn't know what to do. The phone was dead when I tried using it. I thought I could put out the fire so I filled up a glass of water and ran to the hallway and tossed the water on the flames. What was I *thinking*? What could one glass of water do?" Brendon paused and ran his fingers through his hair. "She kept screaming, and I yelled at her to run to me. She wouldn't. She was too scared. It was so hot, flames were everywhere, and I was coughing and having a hard time breathing. I couldn't get to her. I told her I was coming." Brendon hung his head. "After that, I don't really know what happened. The next thing I knew I was in an ambulance, my mom was next to me, crying. She wouldn't say anything when I asked where Julie was."

"Oh, Brendon. I'm so sorry. You can't blame yourself.

186

You were only ten."

"That's what my parents told me over and over. My family was never the same after that. I blame myself and I wonder if I could have done something different."

"Why? The fire wasn't your fault was it?"

"No. It was started by a bad wire in the attic. It doesn't matter. I should have broken a window or gone into the room, or used a garden hose. I don't know, although I do know it's the reason for my nightmares. Sometimes I don't want to go to sleep because I know the nightmares will start again."

"I think talking about it will help your nightmares," Allison said.

"I don't know," Brendon said. He sounded defeated. "It's been hard to accept it, and it's something that I've lived with all my life. I hoped something good would come of it, and it's one of the reasons why I became a police officer. To help people. I never expected to..." He caught himself before he divulged too much.

"To get shot," Allison said, finishing his sentence.

"Yes, that's it." Abruptly, Brendon got off the couch and went over to the window. He didn't like lying.

Allison followed him and put a hand on his shoulder. "Those scars on your chest are from being shot, aren't they?"

Brendon didn't know how to answer.

"I noticed them when we went skinny dipping. Even in the dark, I could see them. I love you, you know that, right?"

Brendon nodded.

"Whatever is eating at you, tell me. You can trust me. Always."

Brendon looked at Allison and opened his mouth, ready to let the words flow, words he had been holding back. When he met her loving eyes, he turned away. "Being shot still does a number on me." He knew he should tell her the rest of the story: that he *was* able to draw his gun, that he *killed* a man, that it was *her husband*. He couldn't lie to her, knowing he owed her more than a lie. His love for her was real. It was right here, right now, and he had never experienced these emotions with another woman, ever.

He couldn't destroy that.

When he looked into her eyes, he saw the depth of her caring, and of her understanding. He had left his old life behind, to search for the woman who he needed to forgive him. He had found something more, something intangible that couldn't be measured or sold or bought, earned only through the mysterious ways of the heart.

"What do you need from me?" Allison finally asked.

"I need you to forgive me."

"I don't understand."

"Just forgive me."

"I do, I will. I'm not sure why you need my forgiveness. If it's what you need, then I do."

Brendon took Allison's face in his hands, this beautiful, strong woman, who he loved and who returned the same love to him. Gently, he pulled her close and kissed her with everything he had, with everything he wanted to give her. He loved her more than he thought was possible. His spirit was reborn, renewed by her forgiveness, and he was more alive than he ever had been. With carnal hunger he kissed her passionately, ardently, running his hands through her hair. He kissed her nose and cheeks, nibbled her neck. In the dimming light, he led her to the bedroom where they made love, and afterwards they talked and laughed. Lying next to her, he traced the contours of her face, up one cheek, down the other with a touch so soft it made her giggle.

"I love you, Allison."

"I love you too, Brendon."

"Marry me?"

Without a second thought or hesitation Allison said, "Yes, I'll marry you Brendon McMahon." She wrapped her arms around him, content in the warm embrace and his strong arms.

Content she would be happy again.

Chapter 24

"Are you seeing this?" Susan asked. She was sitting on the sofa in Allison's shop, sipping a cup of coffee. The TV was turned to a local weather station. "Temps are going to be over a hundred today. Plus there's another wildfire in the Lost Pines state park."

"That explains the smoky haze." Allison was sitting at her sewing table, a flowing pink organza bridesmaid dress draped over the side. She sniffed once. "And that smell. I thought they had those fires under control."

"They did until this new one popped up. The whole area is dry as a tinder box. This is the worst drought in recorded Texas history, and if that fire gets out of control, this whole place will go up in flames."

"Don't talk like that, Susan. My house isn't far from the state park. Besides, I thought there was a tropical storm in the Gulf. Shouldn't that bring us some rain?"

"Don't think so. It looks like all the rain will be east of us. All we're going to get is wind."

"I wondered why it was so windy." Allison paused. "Hey, do you mind if I change the subject to something happier?"

"Go for it."

"Brendon and I are getting married."

Susan nearly spewed the coffee she was drinking all over the floor. Dumfounded wouldn't aptly describe her emotion. "You're *what?*"

"Getting married. I've been meaning to tell you, but it's been so busy, and I've got all these bridesmaids dresses to alter." Allison stopped sewing, overwhelmed at the yards and yards of pink organza overflowing the sewing table onto the floor. "I've been working on them for two weeks. Sometimes I wish people would buy the right size then I remind myself it keeps me in business."

"Who cares about the dresses? This calls for a celebration!" Rising from the sofa Susan declared, "I'm going to get us a drink."

Allison waved her off. "None for me, I'm feeling a little queasy," she said, holding her stomach.

"Party pooper." Susan plopped down on the sofa. "Was it something you ate for breakfast?"

"I skipped breakfast. Didn't have time."

"Oh for heaven's sake, you have to eat. You're going to dry up and blow away if you don't eat. You're skinny enough as it is. I'm going to get you a sandwich and bring it over. Or send Josh to get you one. Where is he?"

"Actually, Josh is on his way here from sleeping over at his friend Carter's house. I called him a little while ago and asked him to bring me a sandwich. Carter's mom said she would stop by the store and then drop Josh over here." Allison checked the time. "Guess they are running late. Josh was supposed to call before he came over."

"What does Josh think about your upcoming nuptials?"

"Josh loves Brendon. I even caught him calling Brendon 'Dad' the other day."

"Wow! This is a big step. Are you ready for this?" Susan asked. "I mean, how long have you guys known each other? A couple of months? You can't possibly know someone enough to marry him in such a short period of time."

"I know enough. I know he's a good, decent man. He makes me laugh, makes me feel alive, like there isn't anything I can't accomplish. I think I knew that from the first time he walked into my store. Remember when he almost bowled you over?"

"Yes," Susan laughed, "I remember. I bet Brendon has been a lot of things in his life, but a bowling pin is probably a new one!"

"I never thought I'd be this happy again. I never thought I could love a man again the way I love him. I think when I married Doug, we were so young and in love, and that carried us a long way. With Brendon, it's different. Quieter I think. More mature. We had a long talk, and he told me things about his childhood that he had never spoken about. He really opened up to me."

"What was it?" Susan asked.

"Childhood tragedy. A fire that killed his little sister." Allison pondered how much to tell Susan, deciding to skip the details. She would be betraying his confidence if she divulged too much, and she wasn't ready yet to talk about the shooting. "He's blamed himself all these years because of it. He was only ten when it happened."

"That's a heavy burden to carry."

"I knew something had been eating at him, but I didn't know what." Allison thought about the things bothering Brendon, especially when he wouldn't finish his sentence, *I never expected to...* What exactly had he meant to say? She had been so caught up in his heartfelt confession and his need for her to forgive him that she forgot to ask about him being shot while on duty. She wondered why he skipped over the details, thinking maybe because it was so close to home, knowing Doug's death was caused by a policeman. Allison didn't hate policemen, yet when she saw a man in blue, a tinge of regret seeped into her soul. They were here to protect people, not take their lives. She supposed she shouldn't judge, never having walked a step in their shoes, though she did understand the risks posed to them every single day like Brendon had told her. Never knowing when he put his uniform on if it would be the last time.

She didn't think of Brendon in those terms, in his uniform, equipment on, patrolling the streets, being shot at. It was a place she wouldn't go to because it would bring back bad memories of Doug's death, and she couldn't fathom the thought of Brendon having to shoot someone, to take someone's life.

Allison thought she was over Doug's death, and had moved on. Lately, for some reason, she kept thinking about that time, and about the policeman who had been responsible. She had to push those thoughts out of her mind or she'd start second guessing her love for Brendon. How well did she really know him was a question she wasn't prepared to grapple with. What did she really know of his old life when he was on the police force? She admitted she had, at times, been struggling with him being a former officer, yet hadn't he left his old life behind and started new? And if Allison could start over, so could Brendon.

"Hey, Earth to Allison," Susan said, waving a hand.

"Huh?"

"You on Mars or something?"

"Sorry, I've got a lot on my mind," Allison said. She reached for the gold locket containing the picture of her treasured daughter.

"You're twirling the locket again. You only do that when you're nervous or when something is bothering you."

"I am?" Allison asked. "I didn't realize I was doing that."

"You want to tell me what's bothering you?"

"I'm tired, that's all."

"Well, I'm glad Brendon opened up to you. When are

the nuptials?"

"In about a month."

"Hmm, I guess Lee Mercer isn't too happy about this. Does he have any idea things moved so fast with you and Brendon?"

"I'm not talking to Lee. We are finished."

"Speaking of people you're not talking to, look who's walking in."

Lee Mercer threw open the door to Allison's shop so hard it hit the wall and jarred loose a hanging picture. He cracked a toothy grin, like the Cheshire cat with a live mouse hanging out of its mouth, toying with its prey before dispatching it.

"Morning ladies," Lee drawled. He was holding a letter size manila folder in one hand, and with the other he picked up the framed picture and set it against the wall. "Sorry about that. Guess I'm a little too excited today."

Susan shot a wicked glare at Lee. "You're not welcome here."

"Nice to see you, too," Lee said. "Frowning doesn't become you, Susan. Makes you look older than you are." He tipped his hat.

"Why you no good–" Rising from the sofa, Susan stepped in between Lee and Allison. "Allie, do you want me to call someone to throw out this trespasser?"

Allison stared Lee down. "No, there are a few things I'd like to say to him," she said indignantly. "Now would be a really good time. Please, Susan, can you leave us alone for a few minutes?"

"Against my better judgment, yes." Walking past Lee, Susan purposely bumped him. She eyed him up and down. "I'll be at the inn, keeping an eye on you."

Lee laughed.

"Ten minutes is all you have, then I'm calling my

husband. He'll be more than happy to make a citizen's arrest."

"Someone might need to be arrested after what I have to tell your friend, but it won't be me," Lee said.

"Maybe me," Susan piped in, "for murder."

"Ooohhh, I'm scared."

"Allie," Susan said, "I'll be back to check on you in ten minutes." Turning to Lee, she said, "I know that look of yours. You're more bloated with gas than a dead whale beached and festering under a hot sun."

"I see you've been looking in the mirror lately."

"You...you, *bastard*," Susan spat. Turning to Allison, her tone softer, she said, "I'll be back."

Allison went to the counter and stood behind it. She crossed her arms and with knives for eyes, glared at Lee. "What do you want?"

"I came here to apologize to you for my atrocious behavior."

"You're lucky I didn't report you and have you arrested."

"I appreciate that you didn't. You know I have a drinking problem, Allison. I wanted you to know I've been going to AA meetings to try to stop. Apologizing to people I've hurt is one of the things I'm required to do in my recovery process. So I'm here to let you know I am truly sorry." He crossed his hands above his heart, patting his chest. "Truly sorry."

"I can't tell if you're being serious or not." Allison studied him for a second. She was dubious of him, especially since he had swaggered into her store like a matador in full costume prancing around in the ring, eager for the kill.

"I *am* serious. Really I am."

"You've said your piece. You can leave now, because as of this moment, we are no longer friends."

"I can live with that. There is one more thing,

though." Lee took a step closer and sidled up to the counter, making direct eye contact with Allison. "I have something for you."

"I'm not interested."

"You'll be interested in this, I promise."

Lee slammed the folder he had been holding onto the counter, and Allison's gaze dropped to it.

"You know that boyfriend of yours?"

"Fiancé," Allison said. She threw her shoulders back in a marked show of defiance.

"Well, then, this gets even better," Lee smirked. He opened the manila folder containing copies of newspaper articles. He held the copies at an angle so that Allison had to crane her neck to see them.

Allison struggled to read the headlines upside down, and couldn't quite decipher the headlines. She did see a grainy picture of a policeman.

Lee shut the folder, satisfied he had gotten Allison's attention and curiosity. "Has Brendon told you he was a policeman?"

"Yes he did."

"In Houston?"

"Yes."

"Did he tell you he got shot while on duty?"

"Yes he did." Allison's irritation showed in voice. "I don't know what you're up to, and I don't have to answer any more of your questions. And what I do or don't know about Brendon isn't any of your business. He's a fine man, more than you ever were or ever will be. We're getting married so you'll have to accept that."

"Maybe so, but before you marry him, I think you'd better read these. You'll change your mind about your perfect fiancé." Lee shoved the folder at Allison then turned to leave. He stopped at the front door. "You can call Susan and tell her I left. By the way, you need to dust these shelves." Lee ran a finger along a glass shelf, brought up his dust covered finger and pointed it at Allison. "It's dirty in here."

"Get out! Now!" Allison screamed. "And don't come back."

Allison fought to keep the bile from rising in her throat. She held her stomach and bent over, reaching for a trash can in case she vomited. She concentrated on breathing and after a few moments, the nausea dissipated.

Holding the folder, she pondered whether or not to open it. Her store was quiet, sans the low mutterings of the news reports about the fire in the state park. She checked the street to make sure Lee had left. She didn't want to give him the satisfaction she was wondering what could be in there that was so almighty important.

With extreme trepidation she opened the folder, and when she saw the picture of the man in blue, she knew immediately who it was.

Chapter 25

Allison's eyes were so teary she had a hard time focusing on the print, and her mind was a muddy puddle of confused thoughts. She read the articles several times, trying to make sense of it all, thinking she must have missed some important fact that would exonerate Brendon in Doug's death. It couldn't possibly be true. *He* was the policeman responsible for Doug's death. How could it be?

She stumbled to her sewing chair, sat down, and laid her head on the pink organza. Something about the smell of fresh material comforted her, and she stretched her arms out, took a handful of the scratchy material, overcome by an unquestionable urge to know the truth.

She tried to bury her senses in the organza, yet the smell of burning timber permeated her store. The haze hung over the city like creepy fog from a Stephen King novel.

Allison concentrated on her breathing and lowering her heartbeat. Otherwise, she thought she might pass out, her emotions running the gamut of an undeniable love for Brendon to one of utter contempt.

His actions were reprehensible.

She mused about the thought he didn't finish: *I never expected to...* "kill someone," Allison said, finishing his sentence.

She thought about his reason for asking her forgiveness, and she knew the reason now. Allison was so lost in thought she didn't hear the jingling indicating the door to her shop had opened.

Brendon walked into Allison's shop holding a Styrofoam container and two drinks. "I brought you lunch."

"What are you doing here?" Allison asked, her voiced laced with anger.

"Whoa. Wait a moment," Brendon said. He was completely caught off guard by Allison's tone of voice. "I brought you some lunch. I wanted to surprise you." He put the container and soft drinks on the counter. "Are you okay? Are you sick?"

Allison didn't answer.

"What's going on?" Brendon stepped closer to her, and put a hand on her shoulder. She recoiled at his touch. "Allison, what's wrong?"

Allison lifted her head. "You lied to me...about why you came here."

"What are you talking about? I came here because I inherited my parents' land."

"Don't lie to me!" she snapped. "It's all here, in this folder." Allison got up, retrieved the folder, and threw it at him.

Brendon flinched when the folder hit him in the chest. It fell to the floor, papers scattering.

Stunned at her outburst, Brendon asked, "What? I don't understand. What is this?" He reached down to pick up the loose papers. He righted one of the papers and his heart plummeted when he read the headline.

"It's all there. All the articles are from the *Houston Chronicle* about how *you* were the policeman who shot and killed Doug during the robbery at the mini mart."

"Allison, let me explain."

"You came here for some sick, twisted reason, didn't

you?" she screamed. "What was it? You had a guilty conscience? Was it some kind of bet you had with your policeman buddies? Oh, I can hear them now." Her voice was mocking when she said, *"Go to her and make her fall in love with you and everything will be hunky dory."*

"It wasn't like that."

"Answer me! What was it?"

"Allie, I—"

"Don't call me that."

"I came here because of you," he said gently. "I came here to ask your forgiveness."

"Oh, and I did that, didn't I?" She glared at him. "Do you think for one moment I'd have anything to do with you if I had known who you were? Why didn't you tell me?"

"I meant to tell you in the beginning, but I couldn't. I couldn't hurt you because I loved you from the moment I saw you."

His voice was calming and reassuring, and for a moment Allison wanted to believe him. "Love based on a lie," she countered.

"No," Brendon said, raising his voice. "I love you with all my heart and soul. If I could turn back the clock I would, and I'd be the one dying, not your husband." Brendon looked at her for a long moment. "Do you know what it did to me? Knowing I killed a man who was only trying to provide for his family? I couldn't go on with my life. I didn't want to live."

"Spare me the pity party. Those scars on your chest are where Doug shot you."

"Yes. I didn't lie to you about getting shot during a robbery."

"Oh, you just left out one important detail like *who* shot you."

"You didn't ask."

"The devil is in the details."

Brendon cringed at the icy rage in her voice. "I meant it when I said I didn't want to live."

"You didn't want to live? Think about me for a moment. I lost my daughter and my husband in the same day. Do you know what that did to me! I wanted to hide from the world, from everybody and everything. I wanted to crawl into a hole and die with them, but I couldn't. I had a child to support, so I picked up the pieces. What did you do? *You* tried to drink your problems away."

"You're stronger than me."

"Is that supposed to make me feel sorry for you? I had no choice. I had to rebuild my life. I had to stay strong for Josh. I had a reason to go on."

"You're my reason to go on now, Allison. I asked you for your forgiveness, and you forgave me."

"That was before I knew you killed my husband."

There was nothing Brendon could say to Allison's revelation.

The tension between them was thick with rage, and during a long lull in conversation, a quiet and tremulous voice asked, "Mom?"

Brendon and Allison whipped around.

Josh was standing near the front door, staring wide-eyed, holding a plastic bag and a drink. He swiveled his attention from his mom then back to Brendon.

"How long have you been here?" Allison asked. Looking at Josh, Allison thought he was about to cry.

"I brought you lunch, Mom. I rode my go-cart all the way here from Carter's house. His mom made you a sandwich." Josh's face was a mixture of confusion and betrayal.

"How long have you been here?" Allison repeated.

Josh didn't answer the question. "You told me Dad died from a heart attack."

"Your dad's heart did stop."

"That's a lie," Josh said, his voice cracking. "He died because Brendon shot him. I heard you say it. When were you going to tell me?"

"Does it make a difference?" Allison asked. "Your dad is gone and is never coming back."

"It makes a difference to me. Why did you lie to me?"

"I was trying to protect you. You were only ten."

"And you, Brendon?" Josh asked. "You lied to both me and my mom?"

"No, Josh, it wasn't like that," Brendon said. "I love your mom and you've become like a son to me."

"I'm not your son, and I never will be! I hate you!" Josh yelled. "I hate you both!" He dropped the plastic bag and drink, pushed open the door, and ran out the store. He hopped on his go-cart and raced away.

"I'll go after him," Brendon said.

"Let him go," Allison ordered. "I'll talk to him."

"Allison," Brendon said, putting a hand on her arm.

"Don't touch me." She wrenched her arm away from him. "Get out. I never want to see you again."

Brendon had nothing to say, so he turned and left the store.

Chapter 26

Brendon stepped out of the store, alone with only a maelstrom of thoughts to keep him company. He aimlessly strolled along the sidewalk, winding his way around the stores along Main Street until he came to the banks of the Colorado River. He took a seat under the same willow tree where he and Allison had kissed.

It was hot and muggy and the smell of distant fires filled the air. A smoky haze covered the entire valley. Nearby, wails of racing ambulances drowned out the gurgling of the languid river. Brendon rested in the shade of the willow tree, feathery strands blowing in the hot wind.

Allison was right. He had lied to her about the real reason for coming to Bastrop. Sometimes he didn't fully understand his reason other than he had an unexplainable urge to seek her out. He thought about Krishna's wisdom and guidance, questioning whether or not it had been the right choice. Still, it was something he was drawn to, something he couldn't find the right words to explain to Allison. All he knew was that he had to ask for her forgiveness.

Knowing she knew he lied to her made Brendon feel dirty, something that the longest shower couldn't wash away. A bead of sweat trickled down the side of his face and he wiped it away with the back of his hand. Looking at the hazy, smoke-filled sky made matters worse, like his whole being was covered in a gray haze.

He hadn't expected to fall in love with her. That was not part of the plan and it had complicated things. If he hadn't felt the need to protect her, he would have told her up front, before she got to really know him.

The revelation was new and raw to Allison and she'd need time to process the knowledge, and perhaps in time she'd understand why he came to seek her out.

All he really wanted to do was to go to her and wrap his arms around her and tell her everything would be okay, that everything would be better in the morning; that they could live happily ever after. He wanted desperately to tell her he loved her, that he loved Josh, and wanted to start a life with her. For her to have his children.

She had every right to hate him, and he had a hard time grasping at how or when she might ever come to terms with it.

He wished she would have listened to him, to let him explain what had happened, that he had no choice but to protect himself and the life of Krishna. Brendon's thoughts went to Krishna and how he had persuaded him to seek Allison out. *When the time is right, the words will be honest and from the heart.*

So much for that.

For a brief moment, Brendon wondered who would have the motive to hurt Allison in such a cruel way, and like a light bulb illuminating a dark room with a flick of the switch, the person and reason was clear. It had to be Lee.

Chapter 27

"Honey?" Susan asked. "What's wrong? You look like something the cat dragged in." Susan came over to Allison who was sitting on the sofa in her shop, and gave her friend a hug.

Allison took one look at Susan and burst into tears.

"Oh, honey, tell me what happened. Did Lee say something to upset you?"

"No, no," Allison said. She dabbed the corner of her eyes with a Kleenex. "Brendon lied to me."

"About what?"

Through bloodshot eyes and a weary voice Allison said, "Brendon was the police officer who shot Doug."

"I don't believe that," Susan said.

"Newspapers don't lie." Rising from the sofa, Allison retrieved the manila folder from the counter and handed it to Susan. "The story is all there, every last detail," Allison said as she returned to sit down next to Susan.

Susan took the folder, opened it, and scanned the papers. "This is awful. Are you sure? I mean, all this can be faked using computers and copiers."

"Brendon confirmed it after I confronted him."

"Oh." It was all Susan could say.

"To top it off, Josh heard the whole thing." Allison uncrossed her legs and reached for another Kleenex. She recounted how Lee had been going to AA meetings; how he needed to apologize for his behavior–to which Susan said "he's still a jerk"–then Allison continued the story, telling Lee to get out; how she read the newspaper copies Lee gave her, ending with the confrontation with Brendon.

"So this is all Lee's doing?"

"I suppose so."

Susan winced. "What did Brendon have to say?"

"He said he came here to ask for my forgiveness because he was so torn up over the shooting." Allison rose from the sofa and went over to the windows at the front of the store, taking in the unusual amount of activity on Main Street.

"Did you believe him?"

"I'm not sure. He said he wanted to die, and that if he could trade places with Doug he would have."

Susan thumbed through the loose pages, speed-reading as fast as she could. "Honey, I don't know if this makes any difference," she said tapping a page. "It says here that Brendon was shot twice before he discharged his firearm. It also says, here," Susan said pointing the passage, "that he was ambushed as he came out of the bathroom."

"What? Why would Doug do that? Why would Doug ambush a policeman? It doesn't make any sense."

"Did you make any follow-up calls to the police department to see if there had been a thorough investigation?"

"No. I didn't want anything to do with any of them."

"Maybe you should make some calls and ask about it," Susan suggested.

"Why? What's the point?"

"Peace of mind."

"Let me see those," Allison said, motioning for Susan to hand her the folder. Allison scanned the passages, taking in as much information as she could. "Brendon didn't mention any of this. I don't know, I can't think, it's too much to process right now."

"Do you still love him?" Susan asked.

"If I didn't love him, this wouldn't be so hard. I told him I never wanted to see him again," Allison said, staring out the window. She furrowed her brow. "Why is it so dark outside?"

Susan let out a big sigh as she sidled up to Allison. "I came over her to tell you that there's been an evacuation order."

"What for?"

"It's all over the news. Haven't you been watching?"

"I've had other things on my mind."

"The fire in the state park has spread and it's heading south toward Highway 71."

Allison gave Susan a look of terror and despair, and clasped a hand over her mouth. "Oh my God, my house...Josh may be in the path."

"Is Josh at home?"

"I don't know. He ran out of here when he heard what happened. The last I saw he was headed north on his go-cart."

"Come on. Grab your purse and let's head to where the town is being evacuated to."

"Where's that?"

"The Walmart parking lot. We'll get a highway patrolman to get Josh."

Chapter 28

A swarm of people mingled in the parking lot of the local Walmart, the main anchor store of the shopping center that was surrounded by satellite stores. A tire store with large plate glass windows covered with posters advertising the latest sales was situated on one end, along with the usual sandwich and yogurt shops, plus two fast-food chain restaurants. The shopping center faced the main freeway running east to west through the town.

Fire-weary residents and confused travelers had been directed to the parking lot where a makeshift command center had recently been set up. Police barricades made sure they didn't cross the bridge spanning the Colorado River because fortunately, the fire had not jumped the river, and for the time being, they were safe.

Heavy, gray, billowing smoke and ash rose up from the ground and into the late afternoon indigo sky, something Allison thought could have been straight out of an apocalyptic movie.

It seemed like the entire Earth was on fire, and the smell of burning timber hung in the air.

Allison had been trying to phone home for hours, terrified Josh was trapped there, yet the land line went unanswered.

Then the 'what ifs' invaded her thoughts like a horde

of army ants tearing and chewing away at her sanity, terrifying her of the possibility that Josh might be trapped in the fire.

The 'what ifs' began to mentally and physically drain her to the point she became dizzy with thoughts that bounced and echoed off the sides of her head as if someone was using her head as a basketball backdrop.

Allison's sweat stained shirt stuck to her back. She breathed fast and shallow, heart pounding, her stomach lurching. She held her stomach, praying she wouldn't toss the meager lunch she had managed to eat.

Normally she had a hearty appetite, and an almost unquenchable sweet tooth, and her friends always teased her that she must have a tapeworm because she could eat like it was nobody's business without gaining a pound. Lately, she had been feeling nauseous morning, noon, and night, but being a single mom and a business owner didn't afford her any extra time to see a doctor. If it continued much longer, she decided a doctor's appointment was definitely in the cards.

She looked around for something to sit on. Slumping over, clutching her stomach, she hobbled over to a cooler full of bottled water someone had placed under the shade of a scrub oak. She collapsed onto it.

"Honey, we need to get you out of this heat." Susan stood back from her friend and brushed the hair back from her face, a friendship gesture, a meaningful one made between friends that genuinely cared for one another. "You look so peaked you could be a cousin to the Jolly Green Giant."

Allison sobbed uncontrollably. "This is no time to joke, Susan. I can't find Josh and he's not answering the phone at home."

"I'm sure he's okay," Susan said, clasping both hands around her cheeks. She fished around in her purse for a Kleenex. "Here, take this."

"Thanks." Allison dabbed her swollen eyes. "Do you have anything for an upset stomach? I'm really nauseous," Allison said holding down the rising bile.

"I think I've got some Pepto Bismol tablets," Susan said. Searching her purse, she found a couple of pink tablets, unwrapped them, and handed two to Allison. "This isn't like you to be this sick. You've got a cast iron stomach."

Allison took the tablets and slowly chewed them until they became foamy, letting the flavor coat her mouth and soothe her flip-flopping stomach. Susan motioned for her to get up off of the cooler so that she could see if there was any bottled water in there. Finding some, she took two bottles, unscrewed the caps, and handed one to Allison.

Allison took a gulp, swishing the remaining crumbly pink tablets from around her teeth. She swallowed, immediately feeling better.

"How long have you been feeling sick?" Susan asked.

"A few days, a week, a couple weeks. I don't remember. It'll pass." Allison waved off the questions she deemed too unimportant to answer. "I probably caught a bug or something."

"Hmm," Susan said. She wondered if it was really a bug, 'or something'. Standing tall, she checked the crowd for Allison's towheaded son. People were huddled in groups, making idle talk with neighbors, and some had gathered around the tent where the authorities were. Kids were running and playing with anything that could be construed as a toy. She did not see Josh. "Have you tried calling his friends' parents?"

"I've been trying to call everybody, including Lee," Allison replied tersely. "The phones are all jammed or down or something. I can't get a signal. And now it'll be dark soon." She paused, thinking about Josh, her tone softening. "Josh will be scared." Allison ran worried hands through her hair.

She took another sip of water and nervously twirled and folded the Kleenex until it had been wadded into a tight square. "What am I going to do?" she asked, pleading with her eyes, hoping her friend would reassure that her only surviving child would be okay.

"I don't know." Susan let out a long sigh. She paused, thinking. "Have you tried Brendon?"

"No," Allison replied, her voice steadfast. "I can't think about Brendon. We're over and that's all there is to it."

"This isn't like you. You're normally the most grounded person there is. I've never seen you like this."

"Like what?"

"So emotional." Susan stopped for a moment, beginning to put two and two together. "Do you think, that you could be, uh..." Susan stopped, afraid to state the obvious. "Being nauseous is a sign of, you know..."

"What?"

"Being pregnant."

"No. I'm not pregnant." Allison hung her head and looked at the pavement. "I can't be. I won't be."

"You are, aren't you?"

"Maybe."

"Does Brendon know?"

"No."

"You have to tell him."

Allison opened her mouth to reply when the crowd gave a collective gasp. Allison and Susan turned in the direction the crowd was looking. A thick black plume of smoke funneled into the air, swirling, twisting like a black tornado of death.

"There went another house," someone said.

"Brendon and I are finished," Allison said with steely determination. "He lied to me the whole time we were together. Do you blame me for not wanting to be with the man who killed Doug?"

"All I know is that you were happy with him, and he with you. I saw the way you two looked at each other at the county fair, the way he held you. And he's good with Josh. Those kinds of men are hard to find."

"He killed my husband. He lied to me the whole time we were dating! How am I supposed to forgive that?"

"I don't know. All I know is that you need to find Josh."

Allison brushed an errant strand of hair away from her face that had been irritating her. "He's okay, don't you think?"

"Josh is a strong, smart boy. He'll be alright. Don't you worry, okay?" Susan said, unconvinced of anything she was saying. She held her friend tightly. Susan looked around, trying to find someone who could offer them hope. A DPS officer was telling residents to stay calm and that the fire probably wouldn't jump the river. "Officer, can you come here a minute?"

The officer excused himself from the group and walked over to Susan.

Susan and Allison started speaking at the same time, and a thousand questions came barreling out of their consciousness. Neither one noticed the tall, lanky man with the piercing blue eyes standing to the side, partially hidden behind an oak growing out of a thin patch of raised dirt. He was fixed on Allison.

"Hold on, slow down," the officer said. "One at a time."

"Officer," Allison pleaded, putting a hand on his arm, "I *have* to go home to check on my son. He's at home and he's not answering the phone." Allison told him where her house was located, about five miles north of the main highway past Dry Creek, around the bend before getting to Lee Mercer's place. She included Lee Mercer in the description because everybody knew where Lee lived. The look on his face was all she needed to know.

"I'm sorry, ma'am. We can't let anyone in there. The winds have shifted from the north driving the fire in the direction where your house is located. It's already close to Mr. Mercer's house."

"What!" Allison screamed, her face a contorted mess. "My son's probably at home! You have to let me go to him!"

"Ma'am, listen to me. The area is barricaded, and we are not letting anyone get through. With the winds blowing from the north and embers jumping fire breaks already in place, it would be suicide if you go in." He paused and lowered his voice. "If you go in, you may not make it out. Do you understand?"

Allison nodded.

"We have fire teams in there, and they need to concentrate on setting a backfire."

"What?" Susan asked. "What's a backfire?"

More people gathered around, mothers holding babies, small children clinging to a parent's skirt or pant leg, worried husbands, and barking dogs in hot cars with windows rolled down.

Soot and smoke billowed angry clouds over the horizon, turning the blue sky into a hellish black. The lanky man dressed in blue jeans and a white T-shirt continued to stand under the oak, unnoticed.

"It's a crew that deliberately sets a backfire to keep the main fire from advancing any further. It's like a road that the fire can't cross. Plus we've got helicopters coming in with flame retardant chemicals that will be dumped on houses that don't have a lot of growth around them." The officer turned to Allison. "Does your house have a lot of shrubs and trees around it?"

"Yes, it does. Why does that matter? Who cares if there are shrubs around my house? What kind of stupid question is that?" she exclaimed throwing her hands in the air demonstrating her frustration. "Haven't you been listening to what I've been saying? I have to go to my son!"

"It matters because the shrubs and trees are fuel for the fire. The more shrubs, the more fuel...you see where I'm going with this?"

"I do."

"Are you sure he's home?" the officer asked. "Maybe he's with his dad."

"His father is deceased. He's home because he had no place else to go."

"Tell me your address and I'll radio the location to the crews working the area. Maybe they can swing by the house, and–"

Before the officer could explain any further, the man in the blue jeans stepped out from behind the tree, pushed his way through the crowd, and cut in on the conversation. "I'll go and find him. I used to be a police officer and I've had fire safety training. I know what to do in these situations."

It was Brendon.

Allison was taken off guard by Brendon's appearance. The last time they spoke, her words had been harsh and swift.

The shock of learning that Brendon had killed her husband, and had purposely kept it from her, was something she didn't think she could ever get over. He'd be like a scar that over time faded from a raw, red mark until only a faint spot was left, then nothing.

"What is your name?" the officer asked.

"Brendon McMahon. I was with the Houston Police Department for ten years and I'd like to help find the boy."

"Are you still with HPD?

"No."

The officer pondered the situation. "I still can't let

214

you in and if you try, former police officer or not, you'll be arrested. Do you understand me?"

Brendon opened his mouth to protest then changed his mind, knowing it would be fruitless because the police had their hands full. "I understand," he uttered. "I'll keep back." Brendon knew he was lying because the last thing he needed or wanted was an altercation that would land him in jail. Best to let the officer think that he would be on his way.

He had overheard the entire conversation when Allison had pleaded with the officer to let her go find Josh. To heck with the question of whether or not Allison still loved him, the heck with everything at this moment, the house, the pine trees, his land, his ancestral home…

Bo!

He remembered he left Bo in the house. He had to find Bo, too. Josh and Bo needed him and he would die trying to save them.

Without wasting any more time, Brendon turned and walked away.

Chapter 29

"Well that's just great!" The sarcasm in Allison's voice was razor-sharp. Forgetting about her topsy-turvy stomach, and the fact that she had almost upchucked her lunch, she turned to Susan. "Did you see him leave? He didn't even have the courtesy to say a polite 'hello' or 'bye' or 'I'm sorry'."

Susan remained silent as she let her friend vent. During the tirade Allison aired every little grievance she ever had, things that in love might have been considered cute, and now were a felony offense.

Misdirecting her anger toward Brendon, she didn't stop to consider the ramifications of what he was doing.

Coward, she thought, standing there watching him walk away.

He didn't even have the decency to inquire how she was doing. Wasn't it obvious by her disheveled appearance that she was in need of comforting right now?

Susan was right. She was pregnant for sure. Her mood swings undulated more than a Ferris wheel at a county fair, and the memories of the morning sickness she had with both pregnancies was something that had been pushed aside, forgotten about, for when her children came along, all the unpleasantness of pregnancies were forgotten. Plus the fact that she was late couldn't be ignored.

For chrissakes, she didn't need to deal with that. And now, Josh was missing. She didn't think she could take any more.

And what did Brendon do? He left without even trying to persuade the officer to let him try to find Josh. Typical of a coward: giving up so easy, not fighting for what was important. Why didn't he fight for her when she pushed him away? Why didn't he try to explain his actions on the day he shot and killed Doug? She had given him ample time to explain, but he chose to walk away leaving her standing in the doorway. She might as well been Scarlet O'Hara standing at the top of the stairs when Rhett Butler said, "Frankly, my dear. I don't give a damn."

Now, *she* didn't give a damn about *him*.

The longer she thought about him the angrier she became. "I hate him."

"No you don't," Susan said.

"I don't need to be told how I feel," Allison said through tight lips. She let out a breath she had been holding, hung her head, and burst into tears, her emotions rolling like a ship caught between swells in a storm lashing its fury. So many conflicting emotions assaulted her. She loved him, she hated him, she loved him, she hated him. She might as well have been pulling petals off a daisy because that was about as fast as her emotions changed from one second to the next.

One minute she would be planning her life with him, living happily ever after in the house with the white picket fence, Bo frolicking in the yard with Josh, the children they were going to have; the next minute she felt manipulated and used.

From the first time they met, she ignored her intuition that whispered to her he had been keeping something from her. If she had known in the beginning who he really was, she wouldn't have given him a second look. What she would have given him was a piece of her mind.

The tears kept coming and she couldn't fight them anymore so she cried openly. How much could one person take? She had remained strong for Josh after the death of Doug and sweet little Madison, and she smiled when she thought of her daughter and her soft skin, cherubic face, chubby fingers, taken at such an innocent age.

A hole the size of the crater blown by the force of the ancient Mt. Vesuvius eruption remained in her soul after Madison died. But like Mother Nature, over time the emptiness had been filled in until Allison found joy in the fond memories. The searing pain had subsided.

When she thought about Doug, she reminded herself that Doug lived on in Josh, and with each passing day, Josh grew to look more and more like his father. Those same hands, lanky legs, the same stride. His voice hadn't yet changed and soon the time would come when Josh would need a father figure. She had thought Brendon would be the father that Josh needed, and for a while, he had been until his secret destroyed their perfect world.

Damn him.

Chapter 30

Walking away from Allison and Susan, Brendon could feel Allison's anger burning into the back of his head like a branding iron, red and hot, scalding his skin. All he wanted to do was hold her and tell her that everything would be alright, feel her skin against his, brush the hair away from her face, tell her he loved her.

With a bullheaded, damn-if-I-care attitude, Brendon kept walking without glancing back, afraid that if he did, he wouldn't be able to leave her. He had to make a plan. Josh's life depended on him.

The two men in dark suits and sunglasses worried him. It was hot and everyone had peeled off any type of constricting clothes so the suits stood out like the proverbial sore thumb. The men had been standing at the command center talking to the people in charge. By the way the computers clicked, it was obvious they were searching for someone.

Brendon looked around for any means of transportation other than his truck that could be easily stopped at the barricades he had seen earlier. The main highway connecting Bastrop to Highway 71 had been blocked by police cars and barricades, one set along the bridge over the Colorado River, the other on the eastbound side of the main highway intersecting the farm-to-market road. Beyond that was the winding road leading to Allison's house. No car could squeeze in between the barricades woven together like a tightly strung braid, but a motorcycle could, and even though it had been a while since Brendon had driven one, he was confident he could handle it.

A motorcycle could top speeds of 120 mph and could navigate the hills and winding roads, and if needed it would be able to outrun a fire even if he had to go off road and into the forest.

Brendon quietly slipped away from the crowd, trying to be as unobtrusive as possible, careful not to do anything that would bring notice to himself. He walked over to the shade of the Walmart and leaned against the brick façade, studying the scene all around him. The parking lot was full of anxious homeowners and wayward shopping carts that had been emptied in haste and left to wander and bump into whatever was in the way.

Cars headed into or out of the shopping center, and while the police were busy trying to calm everybody, Brendon saw his chance.

A motorcycle had been left unattended, keys still in the ignition, and its owner milling at the edge of the crowd, all with their backs to Brendon, all listening intently to what the authorities had to say.

Everyone was oblivious to the man sprinting full speed to the Harley.

His long legs gained on the concrete yardage, the motorcycle was the goal line, Josh's life his cheering section. Triumph was only seconds away.

In one leap, that could only be described as brilliant, athletic, Hollywood stuntman worthy, he came up to the motorcycle, swung his right leg over the seat, grabbed the handle bars, kicked hard on the starter, and revved the engine to life.

Like an untamed mustang that had had a rope

wrenched tight on its hindquarters, the bike bucked to life.

The sound of the roaring engine caught the attention of the motorcycle owner. He saw what was happening, and his momentary indecision gave Brendon just enough time.

"Stop!" he shouted.

In the chaos of the situation, the command garnered the attention of the men in suits.

The owner of the bike waved his arms, ran to his bike, only to be met by flying gravel, squealing tires, and the realization he could do nothing to stop the man who had stolen his bike. He stood there uncertain what to do, perplexed, mouth hanging open. He looked like a deer in headlights, the quizzical expression on his face quickly turning into a *I-can't-believe-this-shit-is-happening-to-me* snarl.

The motorcycle owner kicked the toe of his boot into the asphalt, loosening a pebble. He picked it up, hurling it in frustration at the man who stole his bike. When the men in suits came up to him, they asked if they knew the man who had stolen his bike.

"His name is Brendon McMahon," Allison interrupted.

"Do you know him?" one of the men asked.

"Yes I do."

"We've been looking for him. Ma'am, I'm detective Peter Bradford and this is my partner, Jeff Church. We are with the Houston Police Department."

"Why are you looking for him?"

"Sorry, ma'am, it's classified, and we are unable to talk about it."

"Is it about the shooting of Doug Hartley?"

The two detectives exchanged wary glances. "What do you know about the shooting?" Detective Bradford asked.

"I'm Allison Hartley, Doug's widow."

After the information sank in, the detectives escorted Allison and Susan to an air-conditioned mobile trailer where a bevy of computers and phones were being manned by FEMA. The detectives confirmed Allison's identity then asked her to sit down at a table. The detectives sat opposite of Allison. Susan stood in the corner, listening intently.

"Mrs. Hartley, new information has been uncovered about the shooting."

"What is it?"

"Let me start at the beginning," Detective Bradford said. "As you may or may not know, there had been turnover in the department at the time of the shooting. Paperwork was misplaced, ballistics weren't completed. The case fell through the cracks."

"Obviously, sloppy work," Allison said.

"Yes, ma'am, and we're sorry about that."

Detective Bradford took a sip of water. "One of the new detectives, actually Detective Church, my partner here, cleaned out the office of the man who was in charge of the case, and when he went through the files he found out that the bullets used in the shooting hadn't all been checked."

"I am the one who found them," Detective Church confirmed. "I requested the crime lab to compare the bullets, because each gun leaves its own fingerprints on the bullets."

"I know, I watch TV."

"Yes ma'am." Detective Church shifted his weight. "When the ballistics report came back, we learned the shooting didn't happen as we earlier thought. The lethal bullet that actually killed your husband did not come from Officer McMahon's service pistol."

Allison's gaze went from Detective Church then to Detective Bradford. "Brendon didn't kill my husband?"

"That is correct."

"How do you know?"

"Through careful detective work and ballistics. We also re-created the crime scene."

"It was almost two years ago exactly."

"Yes, ma'am. We had to wait until a couple of weeks ago, so we could recreate the weather conditions as they were on that day. We also made a thorough sweep of the Stop-N-Shop Mini-Mart and that's when we found a round fired from Office McMahon's service pistol lodged between pipes in the attic of the mini mart." Detective Bradford took a deep breath. "There's more."

"Go on," Allison said.

"Ballistics indicates a bullet from Officer McMahon's service pistol hit your husband in the arm, while a different bullet caused the death of your husband."

"Then who was responsible for my husband's death?"

"It was gang related. We compared the bullets to a recent armed robbery nearby and that's when we made the connection. We also reviewed old surveillance tapes from nearby stores around the time of the shooting. Fortunately, those were still in police storage. We asked the FBI to enhance the tapes and that's when we determined two things. First, we could see that the same car was used, and secondly, and most importantly, the man responsible was caught on tape entering the mini mart."

"I don't understand. The owner of the store indicated only my husband was involved."

"The eyewitness didn't actually see the shooting. When your husband came in, he asked for a pack of cigarettes, which the owner said were still in the carton under the counter. He was bending down to retrieve them when the shooting started."

"Doug was trying to quit smoking."

"Right. The owner was behind the counter when the

shooting started, so he assumed it was your husband shooting. We checked bank records and discovered your husband withdrew $30 that morning. We think your husband had been followed from when he used an ATM that morning."

"He was killed over $30?"

"I'm sorry," Detective Church said. "There's more."

"I can't believe this," Allison said.

"The bullets that struck Officer McMahon came from the gang member's gun."

"What?" Allison asked. "I thought my husband shot Brendon."

"No. We think that when the gang member came in, Brendon didn't see him due to the location of the men's room and the fact that the sun was so strong that morning. The glare of the sun blinded Officer McMahon. We also think when your husband pulled his gun—"

"He had a permit to carry a concealed weapon," Allison cut in.

"Yes, we know that. We think your husband recognized he was about to be robbed so he pulled the gun out at the same time Officer McMahon came out of the men's room. Officer McMahon could only see your husband with the gun, and when Officer McMahon was shot, he *would* have thought it was your husband who had shot him. He could not see the gang member because of the blinding sun."

"What about my husband? You said his gun indicated it had been fired. Where did the bullets go?"

"We found them across the street, embedded in a tree. Recreating the scene, we determined that your husband fired two shots at the gang member, both were high and the trajectory of the bullets indicated they went straight out the door and into the tree. Unfortunately, the gang member pulled the fatal shot that killed your husband. He also shot Officer McMahon twice."

"Oh my God," Allison whispered. She hung her head. "So my husband didn't rob the mini mart?"

"That is correct. Your husband was simply in the wrong place at the wrong time."

"We have to tell Brendon. We have to find my son, too."

Chapter 31

Brendon breathed a sigh of relief. The men in suits weren't following him. A stolen motorcycle would be the last concern of the police during the fiery apocalypse, because lives had to be saved. Recovering stolen property could and would wait.

At least he thought so.

He weaved in and out of cars in the parking lot that were inching forward like a logjam on a swiftly moving river. Tunnel vision took over and he had his eyes on the throughway that would lead him to the feeder road then to the freeway. He didn't notice the car barreling to the exit.

Holding tight to the handlebars, trying to control the bike, Brendon nearly jackknifed into the car. He swerved, narrowly missing the car, hit a concrete curb, and bounced over it with such force that he lifted off of the seat.

Fighting to control the bike, he ran up onto the grassy median and tried to duck under the low hanging branches on a tree. His timing was off and a branch full of spiky leaves slapped his face, drawing blood and leaving a striated red welt along the side of his face. In his adrenaline-charged state, he didn't even feel the knobby branch break his skin.

A siren wailed behind him, and for a moment

Brendon thought a police car might actually be coming for him. In the mottled shade of an oak, he stopped the bike on the grassy median and planted both feet on the ground. He assessed his situation. Behind him, two Department of Public Safety officers in their sweat-stained khaki uniforms ran to him, one holding down a service revolver in the gun belt, the other barking commands into the black communication device.

Whatever they were saying couldn't be good, and Brendon had been wrong thinking they wouldn't notice the stolen bike. The two men in suits were running behind the officers.

"Shit!" he spat. "For a stolen bike? Come on!" He couldn't imagine what was so important that four men were now chasing him.

In front of him lay the entrance to the freeway he estimated to be about fifty yards away, and after that where the inferno crackled and hissed, flames licking the sky, devouring the land. Josh was trapped somewhere in that hell.

It was now or never.

If he waited any longer he'd be hauled off to jail, and no amount of fast-talking or the chance of getting a lenient judge who would understand his plight would change anything.

Brendon tilted the bike's handlebars in the direction of the ramp and, grabbing the throttle, he opened it wide and the bike jolted to life, inadvertently doing a wheelie. Just in time too, as the tires squealed dust and grass into the eyes of the two mad-as-hell DPS officers and the clowns wearing dark suits.

The bike roared along the road.

A siren wailed behind him, and the agility and driving capability of the DPS officer following him surprised him, yet no sedan could catch a motorcycle on an open road and Brendon decided to make good use of the concept.

The freeway overpass cutting through Bastrop was nearly deserted except for a few morbidly curious people standing on the shoulder, mesmerized at the fire's wrath of gray smoke billowing in the sky.

Brendon turned right onto the feeder road then guided the bike to the freeway's onramp.

Time to see what this baby could do.

By the time the people milling along the side of the freeway noticed the motorcycle, it was too late. Brendon had raced by like a high speed train, and the wailing sirens became fainter and fainter.

Like a scene out of a James Bond movie, Brendon raced down the freeway, riding the bike like it was part of him.

The sight in front of him was truly apocalyptic.

The verdant rolling hills, interspersed with stands of century old oaks and majestic pines of the Colorado River valley lay directly in the path of the raging fire. The blue-black smoke racing across the valley was something he'd never forget. The stars and stripes of an American flag waved in the hellish wind. It was more like an apocalyptic painting conjured up by an artist spurred on by use of a hallucinogenic drug.

To his right, homeowners in the new housing development scurried about hosing down their houses. Trucks darted in and out of the hardware and grocery stores, the drivers blindly hoping others would not run into them.

Ahead of him, yellow and black police barricades and cruisers were parked to block anyone trying to cross the bridge. Cars that could go no further were idling next to the concrete barrier on each side of the three-lane highway. Owners were chitchatting with each other, some were on cell phones, some were taking pictures, while others sat in their vehicles, air-conditioning running and windows rolled up, oblivious to the life and death scene unfolding right before their eyes.

Brendon stopped in the middle of the freeway, gauging his chance of success at getting through. If the bike crashed that would be the end of the rescue attempt; he could try to talk his way through, explaining that he had been a police officer, knowing the fraternity of brothers transcended from department to department. With little time to waste, he decided his only chance was to barrel through full throttle.

Gripping the seat tightly between his legs, Brendon gunned the engine as a Bastrop police cruiser came up to him, trying to bump him. They were about a second too late.

The bike roared down the freeway, 50 mph, 75, 85, the police cruiser hot on his tail.

Local police officers were waving him off, away from the barricades, demanding that he stop. Brendon ignored their instructions.

He throttled full speed ahead and came to an abrupt stop a few feet away from the barricades, sliding the bike and shuddering it to a stop.

The officer's driving skill wasn't up to snuff to keep up with a motorcycle. The guy clipped the bumper of a stopped car, overcorrected, and hit the concrete divider with such force that the hood popped open and the car's rear wheels lifted off of the pavement.

The officers guarding the barricade stood in awe of the collision.

It could have been much worse, like crumpled dead bodies and missing limbs. As it was, the officer involved in the crash only sustained a minor bump and some seatbelt rash, not to mention a bruised ego.

Brendon saw his chance. He weaved the bike to the left, then right while the officers made mirroring moves, and like any good NFL running back, the best faker won.

Chapter 32

Finally, Brendon was through the logjam of police cars and barricades and back onto open road where the Harley triumphed with its 850 horsepower engine. He raced along the bridge spanning the Colorado River, gunned the motorcycle up the hill, and passed the drought-stricken landscape.

The fire had not reached the divided highway, yet Brendon knew it would only be a matter of hours before the pines would be engulfed by the orange inferno.

At the top of the hill, he slowed the bike, bringing it to a complete stop. He planted his feet on the pavement, taking time to assess the situation.

From what the police had said at the command post in the Walmart parking lot, winds were pushing the fire south. Currently the fire was in the shape of a triangle with natural firebreaks of a divided highway to the north, and the Colorado River to the west. Nothing prevented it from spreading to the south where Allison's house was, and with the fire spreading at a power-walk pace, he didn't have any time to waste.

All he could think about was Josh.

Hugging the Harley, Brendon turned away from the scene in the valley and commanded the bike to gobble more of the road where it diminished from a smooth blacktop to a bumpy red dirt road. Towering pines thick with vines and undergrowth lined the road. Heaps of cinder-dry pine needles lay in clumps alongside the road, kindling waiting to ignite. Bumping and at times sliding, Brendon struggled to control the Harley.

He figured it was about another mile to Allison's house.

It was hot, visibility nil, and Brendon drove with caution.

Seconds ticked by, black soot clogging the air. He coughed the tiny particles out of his lungs. The fire had burned off whatever little humidity was in the air, and Brendon found it was becoming harder and harder to breathe.

Soon the sun would set and he prayed he would find Josh before that. What little ambient light there would have been from the moon would be blocked out by the smoky haze. The time on the bike gave Brendon an opportunity to think about things he had pushed out of his mind. The further he rode, the slower he went, navigating the treacherous potholes. Apparently, this road was not on the county grader's radar.

The heat, his heightened emotions, and the tree canopy enveloping the road lulled him back to a time he had tried to forget, and to the nightmare invading his dreams.

Snippets and flashes of the nightmare clouded his vision as the bike bumped along the dirt road.

He wiped the sweat beading on his brow, his heart thumping harder in his chest.

He thought about Allison and how she told him to leave.

He thought about Josh being alone, the raging fire all around.

Brendon slid the Harley to a stop, letting the engine idle. It all made sense to him now: the shooting, Krishna's words of wisdom, falling in love with Allison.

His purpose in life was to save Josh.

With steadfast determination, he wouldn't let the nightmarish fire of his past win. He'd save Josh or die trying.

He rubbed the soot out of his burning eyes, straining to listen for the sounds of human habitation. He only heard the crackling fire and falling timbers while nocturnal animals fled in the opposite direction he traveled.

The fire was gaining intensity. That much he was sure by the eerie glow of orange imprisoning the sky.

Brendon turned his head in the direction of a faint cry, listening. He thought he heard it again but wasn't sure. Was he imagining it? Had he lost his mind, thinking back to the fire of his childhood where his sister screamed for him? He banged a hot palm on his forehead.

Focus!

Find Josh.

Spurred into action, Brendon throttled the bike and it devoured distance as easily as a ravenous man gulping down food.

It didn't take long to reach Allison's house.

Coming to the gravel driveway, he turned in, killed the engine and bounded up to the house, yelling for Josh. Brendon threw open the screen door and it banged against the wooden side. He fiddled with the locked door and when it wouldn't open, he forced it open, splintering the wooden frame.

"Josh! Josh, are you here?"

He took a glance at the kitchen. Tidy counters, a kitchen table set for two that evening, dishwashing soap placed neatly behind the faucet. He took a few steps and plowed down the hall to Allison's room. It looked normal, serene, the ambient light filtering through the sheer curtains. He checked Josh's room containing a single bed, dresser, baseballs, mitts, clothes scattered about the room.

"Damn it, Josh. Where are you?" Brendon said. He balled a fist and pounded a wall.

He raced outside and stood on the porch, surveying the situation. He pulled in a big breath of air, sputtering and coughing out some soot that had collected in his lungs.

He pulled his cell phone out of his back pocket and dialed 911, but with all the smoke and haze and clogged lines, his call did not go through. He clicked it off and slid it back into place.

Brendon hadn't passed a single car once he had turned onto the road leading to Allison's house. Had everyone evacuated? Maybe Josh been picked up by a neighbor, and in the chaos of evacuation gone somewhere else.

The smell of burning timber permeated the air and every pore of Brendon's skin. His white T-shirt had turned gray, sweat trickling down his back, and his jeans stuck to his legs. The haze of destruction began to cloud his vision and if he didn't leave soon, he'd be meeting his maker sooner than he'd planned.

Winds fueled by the fire whipped the towering pines lining the country road, and smoke rose higher and higher into the darkening sky.

Night had come early.

The majestic oak holding the tree swing bent and groaned under the force of the wind lashing and slashing at the branches, breaking them like matchsticks in a children's game.

A large branch from the oak came crashing down, hitting the dirt, and dust and leaves bounced up into the air, swirling in a wind funnel. Brendon winced and automatically ducked, hunching his shoulders at the crunching and crashing sound.

A loud explosion rocked the countryside, sending a tsunami of fiery air propelling burning dust and leaves, soot and red hot embers. The road acted like a tunnel, funneling the fireball at breakneck speed.

He waited until the fireball evaporated, and sensing time was of the essence, he jumped on his bike, revved the engine, and turned away from the house and out onto the road where he came to an abrupt stop.

Towering, angry flames engulfed the road leading to the main highway, cutting off his escape in that direction, the fireball having ignited the cinder-dry land. He coughed and desperately sucked in what little oxygen remained.

He gauged his chances of escaping through the countryside, mulling over the barbed-wire fences cutting through the tracts of land, thinking the motorcycle would be useless. He cut the handle bars to the left, swung the bike around, and headed in the opposite direction. By now the smoke had blocked out light. The headlight illuminated the land in an eerie foreign haze, like Brendon was in a mini-submarine in the dark depths of an ocean, the light highlighting a stream of particles, suspended in animation.

Visibility was almost nil. The soot stinging his eyes, fire crackling around him, he drove slowly, hugging the side of the road, knowing if he missed a turn he could crash the bike and end up with a broken leg or worse.

Through the haze he detected movement, the shape slowly coming into focus, and he couldn't believe his eyes!

It was Josh racing along the road in the go-cart, Bo running alongside of him, panting and tongue hanging out.

"Josh!" Brendon yelled. He stopped the motorcycle. "Josh!"

Josh snapped his head up, scanning the road trying

to identify where the sound was coming from, and when he saw Brendon, he gunned the go-cart heading straight toward him. Bo raced alongside of Josh. When they came to Brendon, Bo plopped down on the ground, panting, his eyes wild with fear.

"Brendon, you're here! You don't know how glad I am to see you. I didn't know what to do. I waited as long as I could at my house and when nobody came I got my go-cart and went to your house, but you weren't there. Bo was scratching to get out, so I let him out. Then I went to Lee's, but he's drunk and wouldn't open the door." He snuck a look at Brendon, and rubbed his red eyes with a shirt sleeve. "We're going to die here."

"No we're not."

"We are," Josh said. His tone was desperate. "Don't you see? The fire is all around us."

"We'll get out," Brendon said. "Don't panic."

"I'm trying not to." Josh looked at Brendon. "Are you mad at me for saying I hated you?"

"No, Josh. That's the last thing on my mind."

"I didn't mean what I said. When I realized my mom lied to me, I blamed you."

"I know. Look, Josh, grownups do stupid things sometimes, things we don't even know we're doing. I meant to tell your mom who I was from the moment I met her. I couldn't though. I'm sorry for what happened, you have to believe me. I never meant to hurt anyone, especially your mom. I love her. I love you like a son. You need to know that."

"Yeah, I guess I know that. Where's my mom? Is she okay?"

"Yes, she's fine. She's with Susan at the Walmart parking lot where people were evacuated to. She's worried sick out of her mind about you. When I heard you were missing, I came to find you."

"You did?"

"Yes! I wouldn't leave you here. Don't tell anybody I stole the Harley."

"That's awesome."

"Yeah, well, maybe not if they throw me in jail."

"How are we gonna get out of here? I want to see my mom."

Brendon rubbed his temples, which were pulsing with each heartbeat, thinking exactly that: *How to escape?*

Darkness had set in, the pines towering black until they disappeared into the night, the wind whipping its fury.

The road ran north to south, and Josh confirmed their escape route to the north had been cut off. They could try again heading south, though it was too risky because the fire had jumped ahead of them, and with the ever-changing wind, the fire could be on them at any moment. While Brendon pondered the situation a crackling sound, deep and guttural, shattered his thoughts. He looked up to see a pine that had been cut in half, jagged bark oozing sticky sap, teetering perilously above them, waiting for a puff of breath to finish it off.

Brendon acted instinctively, jumped off the bike, and looped an arm about Josh, whisking him off the go-cart without giving the boy time to protest.

Bo darted in the opposite direction.

In a whoosh of air and dust and pine needles and flying embers, the massive tree crushed the go-cart crumpling it into broken pieces of metal.

Brendon and Josh sprinted with lightning-fast speed down the road, stumbling into a ditch where he released his hold on Josh. They tumbled into soft ground and when Josh regained his senses, he curled into a little ball and covered his head with his arms. Brendon scrambled over to where the terrified boy lay and hurled his body on top of Josh to protect him from whatever nature was throwing at them.

Brendon's heart was pumping so fast he thought it would burst out of his chest. He concentrated on breathing and lowering his heartrate.

In the darkness, Bo barked somewhere.

"Bo!" Brendon yelled. "Over here. Come, boy! Here!" Brendon cocked his head to the side listening intently and focusing solely on keeping them together.

Smoke swirled around them and Brendon coughed. Lifting his head he yelled more forcefully, "Bo!" Much to his relief, Bo padded through the brush, shaking, tail tucked, whimpering. When he came up to Brendon and Josh, he licked their faces with long wet licks.

Josh wiggled out from under Brendon and grabbed Bo and hugged him, stroking his head and running his hand down the ruff along Bo's back. "It's okay, it's okay," Josh kept assuring the petrified and heavily panting dog, talking to him in a soothing voice like a mother comforting her child.

"We've got to get out of here," Brendon said.

"How? The fire has cut us off."

"If we stay here, we'll die. Let's start moving."

"It's so dark I can't see anything," Josh protested. "Which way should we go?"

"Let's head back to your house, it's only about a hundred yards that way," Brendon pointed. "We'll take the motorcycle to your house then ditch it and...and..."

"And what?"

"I don't know, let's get going."

Brendon, Josh, and Bo scrambled out of the ditch, their feet sliding on the blanket of dry pine needles, trying to get traction. If anyone could have seen Brendon and Josh, they would have thought they were refugees from a war torn country. Faces and arms darkened with soot, a long tear had appeared in Brendon's shirt, dirt encapsulated his jeans, their expressions haggard and body language even more so.

When they reached the road, Brendon stopped dead in his tracks.

Sensing something was wrong, Josh asked, "What's wrong?"

Brendon let out a sigh, bemoaning his luck that the motorcycle was now a useless hunk of twisted metal thanks to the pine tree. The biggest part of the pine had smashed it, bending it like it was a pliable piece of clay.

"The motorcycle. It's useless. There's no time, let's get to your house. Are you hurt? Can you run?"

Josh shook his head. "Yeah, I can run. Fast too," he added proudly.

"Excellent. Let's go." Brendon whistled for Bo, who trotted up to them. First a few steps, then more as feet then yards fell behind them. Bo had raced ahead of them sensing the run had purpose.

It was dark, the only light coming from the flames leaping in the air. Long streaks of smoke curled upwards into the darkness, pale orange glowed at the topmost leaves of the pines, and the leaves whispered their despair. Shadows lingered under the brush and the pines, long fingers reaching out in loneliness toward the man, boy, and dog who ran, their footsteps heavy on the road.

Finally, they reached Josh's dark house. Unknown to them, electricity had been cut off by the electric company.

The fire raged and crackled around them, hissing death in every direction, cutting off escape except for one narrow corridor.

"Does your mom have any flashlights?" Brendon asked.

"I don't think so. She has candles. Would that help?"

"No, they wouldn't." Brendon paced back and forth on the crunchy, dry grass, thinking, searching for anything that might help. "Do you have a land line?"

"A what?"

"It's a phone that plugs into the wall."

"Um, I think so. I think it's the phone in my room. My mom said if there was ever an emergency I should use that phone."

"Doesn't matter. Let's go."

Taking the porch stairs two at a time, Brendon was on the porch in no time flat with Josh and Bo bringing up the rear. He threw open the door. It was dark and stuffy in the house. He padded across the living area, down the dark hall, his hands running along the wall, and when he got to the doorway into Josh's room, he swung in.

"Where's the phone?" Brendon asked breathlessly.

"Probably on the floor somewhere," Josh said.

Brendon crawled on his hands and knees, sweeping the floor looking for the phone. He pushed away a couple of footballs, an old pair of tennis shoes, and some dirty clothes. His fingers reached through the clutter until he located the phone. "I found it!"

He put the handset to his ear. There was no dial tone. He jiggled the clear cylinder-shaped plunger several times, brought the handset to his ear and listened again for a dial tone. "Shit," he said, "It's not working." He looked at Josh sitting on the bed, cross-legged, covers pushed down from the pillows, petting Bo. "When was the last time you used this phone?"

Josh shrugged. "I don't use it because the only people who call are telemarketers. My mom said to unplug it."

"Of course," Brendon said, understanding why the phone didn't work. He held the phone cord in his hand, pulling it through until he reached the end. "Where's the plug?"

"Behind my dresser."

Bending down on a knee, Brendon ran his hands

along the wall behind the dresser until he found the wall plug and contorted his body, squeezing his arm behind the wooden dresser. Fumbling with the cord, he plugged it into the outlet.

Letting out the breath he had been holding, he listened for a dial done. "Yes!" he exclaimed, pumping his fist into the air. He dialed 911 and waited for the operator. When one answered he gave her the address and their dire situation. The 911 operator looked at the latest fire map on her computer with fire icons dotting the screen, indicating entire swaths of land burning.

When Brendon's location popped up on her computer monitor, she let out an audible "Oh dear Lord". On the screen, fire icons increased and merged together in a big blur, blinking glowing red. "Sir, are you still there?"

"Yes," Brendon answered.

"You need to leave *now*. Head east, then north."

"There's no road that way, only forest." Brendon was becoming worried as he pictured the land in his mind. Tangled brush, sometimes so dense it was impenetrable, and miles of forest and hills of a wild and untamed land.

"Sir, the fire has merged all around your location except for a narrow, linear line in a north/south direction." The operator leaned back in her chair, closed her eyes and said a silent prayer. "It's your only chance."

"Hello? Hello!" Brendon yelled. He jiggled the plunger several times, realizing the phone had gone dead. "We've got to leave now. Where are the towels?"

"In the bathroom, why?"

"We need to wet them down so we can cover our faces from the smoke. We'll need one for Bo too. Josh, do you have one thing you'd like to save?"

"Yes, I do," Josh said after a brief pause. "A picture of my dad."

"Get it then and let's go."

Josh rummaged through the top of his dresser, found

the picture, and he, Brendon, and Bo raced out the back door. Down the steps they ran, out the gate of the back fence, pushing through the brush as the flames licked the yard of the house.

Three lives alone in the blackness, running, stumbling, coughing the soot from their lungs. The terrain was unfamiliar to Brendon and he quickly became lost. Was he going north, or maybe it was east? He did not know. Behind them the fire gnawed and ravaged the countryside, turning trees to blackened stubs, roads covered in ash, houses now reduced to black smoke and charred memories.

Everything was hazy.

Panting and out of breath, Brendon stopped. Stooped over, hands on knees, he held the wet towel to his face. Bo came over, whimpering, and Brendon did the same for his loyal pet. Josh stopped and did as Brendon was doing.

"I think we're trapped," Brendon said.

"Are we going to die?" Josh asked as only a child could, not quite comprehending the finality of death.

"I don't know." Brendon sputtered and coughed. "I don't know which way to go. I'm completely turned around."

Josh coughed.

"I'm not going to leave you, Josh."

The solemn moment between Brendon and Josh seemed to finalize their dire situation. The darkness, the glowing fire, crackling, moaning. Josh hung his head in defeat. Bo nuzzled Brendon's leg.

Brendon put his arm around Josh to protect him. "I'll love your mom and you until I die."

Josh nodded.

Breathing became difficult, and Brendon's thoughts harkened back to the time he and Allison had skinny dipped in the spring-fed pool. If he was going to die, he wanted to remember the woman he loved. He pictured her in his mind, her flowing hair, sparkling eyes, and what they had said to each other...

A strange feeling came over Brendon, one of complete acceptance of love, something so strange he thought he might be having an out of body experience, either that or he was already dead and in Heaven.

Things moved in slow motion: Bo barking, Josh talking, the wind, the crackling noise. His mind searched for meaning, but before he could grasp it, Bo barked loud and throaty.

"Now's not the time," Brendon said. "I'm sorry, Josh. There's no place for us to go."

Woof!

Bo bellowed long and mournful, head raised at the sky.

"Maybe he's trying to tell us something," Josh said.

"He probably senses our time is over."

"No, he's looking at something. He's looking at the sky," Josh said.

Brendon studied Bo and followed his eyes to the sky as a thought came to him: What had Madison said to Allison before she died? *Look to the stars.*

That's what Brendon did. He lifted his gaze at the darkened sky, his eyes burning and stinging. He rubbed his eyes, and like Moses parting the Red Sea, the smoke cleared and stars shined brilliantly in the night.

"The North Star!"

Brendon tugged on Josh's shirt sleeve.

"That's our way out of here, Josh! Madison said to look to the stars."

The brilliance of the North Star beckoned to them, willing them to move, to fight. He and Josh got up, running through the countryside, dodging embers and death, the North Star guiding them to safety. Bo was a step behind them. When at last they came upon a pond, they waded in, laughing and high-fiving. Bo dogpaddled to a boulder where he collapsed.

They had survived.

Chapter 33

Through the fog of a drunken stupor, Lee gradually woke. He was in his La-Z-Boy recliner. An empty bottle of whiskey had slipped out of his hand and had fallen askew onto the floor.

It was the smell that hit him first, and Lee thought some bozo had managed to start a grass fire, although grass fires didn't sound like a freight train barreling at full speed.

Squinting through the hazy, soot-covered windows, he wasn't quite sure he was seeing correctly. The orange glow worried him and he rubbed his red eyes. At first he thought his eyes were playing tricks on him, or maybe it was the whiskey. He remembered polishing off the whiskey he had bought earlier in the day, swearing this would be his last binge.

Rising from the recliner, he stumbled over to the front door and threw it open, and a blast of fiery heat hit him in the face. He struggled to catch a breath.

The scene was incomprehensible, and he tried to make sense of it.

The sky was dark and waves of dense smoke blew over the land like towering thunderclouds, the grass was blackened and smoldering, angry orange flames steamrolled forward, devouring trees and brush. Crackling and hissing, tornadoes of flames swirled in the wind, lashing against the land.

The noise was deafening.

Lee stood there aghast, mouth open as the living, breathing inferno barreled down upon his house. The fire's fury was unmerciful and unforgiving of anything too weak or slow to escape.

A red fox squirrel, its eyes filled with terror, tail swishing in panic, clung to a smoldering pine tree near Lee's house. Always an opportunist, the squirrel refused to relinquish an acorn it was holding in its mouth. Even in the inferno, the squirrel's ingrained instinct guided him to keep the nut for later dining.

Chattering, the squirrel contemplated how to escape as it watched the human emerge from the house.

In a momentary reprieve from the deadly fire, the squirrel scampered down the pine tree, darted across the burnt ground, then skittered up to the porch where Lee was standing. It had lost all fear of humans. The squirrel let go of its prized acorn, which clattered and bounced around on the porch. When the acorn came to a rest on one of the steps, the squirrel latched onto Lee's pants legs, climbed halfway up, and clung to him for dear life.

Lee screamed and shook his leg trying to loosen the squirrel's death grip.

The frightened squirrel climbed higher, digging its claws into Lee's back, then his scalp. Sitting atop Lee's head, its bushy tail swished back and forth, smacking Lee on his face, momentarily blinding him while little claws dug into flesh, dark eyes bulging with panic.

Drops of crimson on Lee's scalp oozed from the puncture wounds.

Lee thrashed around on the porch, his hands trying to loosen the grip the squirrel had on him, and in the melee of confused human and terrified squirrel, the scene could have been out of a Laurel and Hardy skit if the circumstances weren't so dire.

In the few seconds Lee wasted flailing around on the porch, the fire had steadily gained ground through the dry brush, engulfing pines as if the trees had been soaked in a flammable liquid. In its fiery wake it left a trail of toppled trees and parched earth, with broken animal carcasses littering the land.

Finally, Lee grabbed the squirrel by its haunches and with a solid grip he launched the terrified animal through the air, past the porch, over the flowerbed where it landed with a thud on the sizzling ground.

With the tip of its tail smoking, the dazed and panic-stricken squirrel did what squirrels do best: it ran for its life, across the ground, scrambled under a fence then bolted to an evergreen oak tree where it took refuge. The agile, uninjured squirrel climbed high in the tree, perched on a branch where it viewed the surrounding inferno.

Flames shot a hundred feet into the air, crackling and hissing like a giant reptilian creature from the bowels of Hell, its sole purpose to destroy every living thing. Smoke filled the horizon, and fire-tinged wind whipped the trees, scorching the land.

The squirrel panted heavily, huddling flat against the oak tree. Without anyplace else to go, the squirrel climbed into a tree cavity it found, curled into a protective ball, awaiting its fate.

"Damn tree rats!" Lee yelled when he saw the squirrel duck into the hole. Holding onto a column of the porch to steady himself, Lee took a deep breath. The heated air singed his lungs and he fell to his knees, clutching his chest and a handful of his shirt. When he took another breath he sucked in more heated, oxygen-starved air.

He thought he was having a heart attack.

He lowered himself on the porch, hoping to find a

pocket of breathable air. He took a few breaths and gasped, realizing if he stayed here he'd die. He fished around in his right pants' pocket for the keys to his truck. Finding them, he let out a little sigh of relief that he had not put them on the kitchen counter like he normally did.

He still had time to escape.

Lee formulated an escape plan, mentally checking a route his four-wheel drive truck would take him. He glanced at the truck, parked where he always left it in what used to be a shady spot under a pine tree, now under attack.

Flames licked the trunk of the tree, steadily rising higher, crab-walking like a gargoyle climbing the walls of a medieval castle. The tree bent and twisted as if trying to shake off an intruder. Helpless to do anything, Lee watched as the tree succumbed to the inferno.

The land and his house would be the next casualty, and so would Lee if he didn't leave now. With newfound determination, Lee decided to take a chance and make a run for it to his truck. If the roads were blocked, he decided he could easily navigate the land, thinking it had been a wise decision to buy a souped-up truck with a four-wheel drive and a high suspension. He'd be able to mow down fences without a hitch.

Garnering his remaining strength, he rose and wiped the stinging sweat from his eyes. Lee took a step on the porch, but in his drunken stupor and haste he didn't see the acorn the squirrel had dropped. Slipping on it, Lee's legs went out from under him, arms flailing in the air, and he awkwardly tumbled down the hard steps, landing hard on his back. The air was knocked out of him and he struggled to breathe. Catching his breath, he went to get up when the most god-awful pain gripped his leg.

His body shuddered, and he screamed and cursed in agony.

Lying still for a moment, breathing shallow, Lee tried to regain his senses. He blinked away his blurry eyesight and commanded his numb mind to work. He had to assess his injury. Gathering what remaining focus he had, he pensively looked at his leg, grimacing at the unnatural, twisted position.

He let his head fall back and pounded the ground, yelling a slew of obscenities, cursing at that damn tree rat and his bad luck.

It was getting hotter.

The fire was all around him, licking at the foundation of house.

In anticipation of pain, Lee gritted his teeth before throwing himself on his stomach. It was all he could do to stay conscious, never having experienced such debilitating and searing pain.

Giving himself a pep talk, he worked through the pain, commanding his arms to propel his body forward. He crawled inch by agonizing inch along the parched ground, his bad leg still at an unnatural angle.

Lee's eyes rolled upward and he sank to the ground, consciousness slipping away. His breathing became labored and each breath felt like a hundred razor-sharp needles were slicing his lungs.

Still, he refused to give up.

"Come on you can do it," he said.

The truck was only yards away, and a newfound strength surged in him.

Willing his scratched and bruised arms, he crawled along the ground at an agonizing pace. He heard a splintering crack, and for a moment he thought the pine tree had sustained a direct lightning strike. It sounded like a bomb had been detonated. Lee instinctively covered his head.

Splintered, sizzling branches and razor sharp pine needles rained down on him, slicing through his shirt and pants. Sap exploded like firecrackers, sending hot missiles of flaming goo in all directions, slapping Lee on the back, burning holes in his shirt and searing his tender skin.

His entire body convulsed with throbbing, burning pain.

When the maelstrom of prickly pine needles and broken branches stopped, Lee cocked his head and looked up. His face contorted into a look of absolute horror.

A massive tree limb teetered precariously directly above him, hanging by a sinew of flaming bark.

He didn't have time to think, to postulate, or to form another plan of action, because in a split second the massive tree limb broke away from the tree.

For a brief moment, Lee understood his body was about to be ravaged by the tree limb as sure as a cockroach would be squashed under the sole of stomping foot.

Flashes of an unlived and unsatisfying life came to him.

In the second it took to crash down, Lee didn't feel the crushing impact of the tree limb; he didn't feel the massive internal injuries and resulting hemorrhaging; he didn't feel his bones breaking; didn't feel his eardrums burst when blood came rushing out.

He only felt blackness and a life wasted.

The land burned during the night, and when morning came the full devastation was revealed. Blackened, smoldering pine trees and great swaths of naked land were stripped of grass and foliage, looking like an atomic bomb had been detonated.

Even in the carnage, life made a valiant stand. Small pockets remained untouched and viable. Random oaks, lizards darting out from their hiding places, birds flying in the sky, winged insects flitting, and the squirrel who had taken refuge in the oak tree emerged.

Sitting on a tree limb, its nose twitching in the air, the squirrel picked up wafting scents of unfamiliar odors of caustic chemicals and burned flesh.

Hunger and curiosity drove the squirrel from the tree. Cautiously it climbed down and padded over to the remnants of a house. The foundation was still intact, the chimney standing, all surrounded by heaps of incinerated walls, house frame, insulation, wooden furnishings, and a plethora of household goods.

A burned shell of a truck sat idle, its tires flattened to the ground, the interior gutted and windows blown out. A once magnificent pine tree lay toppled on the ground, and a strange shape with a repugnant odor the squirrel could not identify lay trapped by the pine tree.

Sitting on its haunches, nose in the air, the squirrel sniffed in all directions, searching for food. A familiar smell captured the squirrel's attention and he scurried over to where it emanated from. The squirrel checked the sky for avian predators, and sensing it was safe, began digging.

Faster the squirrel dug, his little paws searching for a prize.

Sticking his nose to the ground, the squirrel found the acorn it had dropped the previous day. He held it securely in his mouth then scampered back to the safety of the oak tree. Sitting at the bottom of the tree, the squirrel crushed the outer shell of the acorn before finding the soft inner part it nibbled on. It was an unusual, not unpleasing flavor, slow roasted by the fire.

After finishing the acorn, the squirrel climbed the tree, sat on a sturdy branch, and groomed its fur, taking care to wash his singed tail. Satisfied at its accomplishment of finding a meager breakfast, the squirrel looked out over the remnants of the once great forest, sniffed the air, and searched for another cache of acorns it had hidden.

Epilogue
Seven Months Later

Allison was thankful for the family she had. On that day when she thought she had lost everything, a DPS trooper had delivered Brendon, Josh, and Bo to her. She collapsed in their arms, hugging them.

She told them about the visit from the two Houston Police Department detectives and how the shooting had actually happened. She cried openly, telling Brendon how sorry she was, how she still loved him, and asked him if he still wanted to marry her. His response was an unequivocal yes.

Less than a month after the fire, Brendon and Allison were married in a civil ceremony witnessed by Josh, Susan, and her husband, Brian. They even had Bo in attendance after explaining to the pastor how Bo was instrumental in saving them. Afterwards, they celebrated by eating dinner at a local restaurant that allowed dogs, as long as they dined on the patio. During the dinner, Bo sat quietly by Brendon's side.

Allison's house had escaped the fiery inferno, although the dead trees around it provided a daily reminder of that dreadful day. In the spring she planned to plant some saplings, and in a few years she hoped they'd have a little bit of the shade that had been lost.

The remodeling to add another bedroom was almost

finished and she'd finally have room for her expanding family.

Brendon's home had been incinerated in the fire. At first he was sad until he realized he could finally let go of the past. He kept the good memories, cherishing the time he had with his sister and his parents. He buried the bad memories in the rubble of the house. He kept the land, leasing it for grazing so he could qualify for the agricultural exemption.

He had a new life now, a wife, a child on the way, son, beloved dog. It was a new beginning for him. He had also decided to go back into police work, applying for and being accepted into the Department of Public Safety, DPS for short. Being a trooper in the DPS filled a need of his to help people that he had missed since he had quit the police force.

It was mid-February, and a cold front had blown in a few days earlier, bringing rain. When the clouds dissipated, the sky was a crystalline blue, the air clean.

Brendon, Allison, and Josh were sitting down at the table eating breakfast.

As customary on Saturday morning, Brendon had made his special omelet with cheese, mushrooms, and spinach, topped with Picante sauce. A bowl of sliced strawberries was available too. He wanted to make sure Allison ate healthy and as much as she wanted to.

Bo sat by Josh, eagerly waiting for a tidbit to be dropped his way.

"Dad, can you drop me off at Carter's house?" Josh asked, scarfing down another bite. "We've got practice at noon and I need to get to his house on time. It's his mom's turn to take us."

"I'd be happy to. Your mom needs to take it easy today."

Allison met Brendon's gaze. She smiled and put her

hand on his.

Josh stuffed his face as fast as he could with the last bite of omelet and washed it down with a swallow of milk. "I'll take a quick shower and I'll be ready in ten minutes." He took his dishes to the sink and raced to the shower.

"Thanks for taking Josh," Allison said. "It was a busy week and I need the rest."

"It's the least I can do for my beautiful wife and baby." Brendon patted Allison's belly. He finished his coffee then cleared the table. "After I take Josh to Carter's house, I'll stop by the store and pick up a paper. Maybe there are some sales we can check out this afternoon."

"Good idea," Allison said. "Honey, I'm too tired to go into my store today. Susan said she would look after it for me."

"Are you feeling okay?"

"Only tired. I'm going to try to get some extra sleep. Would you mind taking Bo with you? I'm going to go back to bed for little while and if Bo's here I'll feel guilty for not taking him on a walk."

"I'll take him with me."

"Dad!" Josh yelled. "I'm ready!" He raced down the hall, grabbed his baseball glove and bat, and was out the door.

"Better get going," Brendon said. "Come on, Bo. Let's go."

Bo trotted after Brendon and Josh. "I'll be back in about an hour."

Brendon drove past the Colorado River, onward past Main Street and the tourist shops, the gas stations, law offices, and various county buildings until he came to the subdivision where Carter lived.

Brendon dropped Josh off at Carter's house and said

the usual pleasantries to his mom. He left and drove out of the subdivision then onto the main highway. He kept thinking about his life and how lucky he was to have found Allison. As he was about to make a turn to go back home, he remembered he forgot to get the paper.

Fortunately, at the next intersection was Buc-ees, a Texas-sized convenience store for travelers, stocked with aisles upon aisles of candy, chips, and drinks, plus an inordinate amount of other Texas goodies. It would also be a good place to let Bo out so he could stretch his legs.

The place boasted the cleanest restrooms of any convenience store, and Brendon, along with every visiting traveler knew this to be the case. Billboard signs advertising *"What's the best reason to stop at Buc-ees? Number 1 and 2"* along with that caricature of an enormous, adorable beaver were placed all along Texas highways.

There was never a line, plenty of soap, diaper changing stations, and the fact that framed pictures depicting serene Texas scenes of bluebonnets lined the walls made it a downright pleasurable experience.

The store, along with the parking lot, play area, dog run, and gas pumping stations, covered several acres on the outskirts of town at the intersection of two busy highways.

He nodded when he thought about the brilliance of getting the market on that concept. Who would have thought that Buc-ees and its buck-toothed beaver seen on T-shirts, caps, and bumper stickers would be as embedded in Texas culture as the ten gallon hat?

Brendon pulled the truck into the parking lot and cut the engine. "Come on, Bo, let's go stretch our legs." Secured with a leash, Brendon walked Bo over to the grassy area where travelers walked their dogs.

Bo had his nose to the ground checking the scents of

all the dogs who had been previously walked. He dismissed them as unknown dogs, except for one. It was a scent that brought back memories of bonding and working together to survive. An image of a small dog formed in his mind and Bo's eyes searched the dog run.

A man and his daughter, who was walking a small white fluffy dog approached them.

Bo lifted his snout, sniffing the air in short, quick bursts. He stood at attention, his tail straightened and he wiggled from side to side. Trying to reach the small dog, Bo pulled hard on the leash, and coughed at the collar tightening around his neck.

"Afternoon," Brendon said to the man and his small daughter. "Nice dog you have."

Bo tugged more on the leash, and Brendon held him back using both hands. Bo struggled so much that he lifted his front paws off the ground.

The little white dog canted her head and looked at Bo. Her nose twitched taking in the smell of the larger dog. And she too recognized Bo as the dog who took care of her at the rest stop.

"Sorry about this," Brendon said. Bo had pulled on the leash making it taut. "I'm not sure what's wrong with my dog. He usually isn't like this."

"Maybe he only wants to say hi to my dog," the little girl said.

Brendon looked to her dad for confirmation.

He said, "I guess it's okay. She doesn't seem afraid like she normally is."

"Her name is Snowflake," the little girl said, petting her dog. "My name is Bailee, and that's my dad."

"Mark Harris." He extended a hand.

"Brendon McMahon. You folks live around here?"

"Moved here last spring. Decided to come live with my folks after my wife died. Needed help raising my daughter."

"I'm so sorry." Brendon's tone was genuine. For a few seconds it was quiet until Bo whimpered. "Wow! I haven't ever heard that. What's wrong with you, Bo?"

"They're trying to make friends," Bailee said. "It's okay. He can meet Snowflake now."

"You be nice, Bo." Brendon loosened the grip on the leash, letting Bo closer.

Bo went to Snowflake and sniffed her. He ran his nose along her face and her back then to her tail. The little white dog with the sweet face and soulful eyes stayed still. Bo nibbled the little dog's ears, grooming her like he used to. Snowflake leaned into Bo, and closed her eyes, savoring the larger dog's tenderness.

As the three looked on in amazement at their dogs' behavior, Brendon could have sworn a brief flicker of some understanding or recognition transpired between Bo and Snowflake. Some sort of a nonverbal communication. He was profoundly moved by it.

"That's the oddest thing I've ever seen. They're acting like they know each other. Where did you find her?" Brendon asked.

Bailee said, "We found her at a rest stop. She almost died, but my daddy saved her." Bailee wrapped her arms around Snowflake and pressed her face into her fluffy fur. "She's my dog now."

"That's right," Mark said. "We found her at that rest stop about an hour's drive east of here. We were on our way here when we stopped there. That's when we found her. It's a good thing because the vet said she only had about a day left."

"How about that," Brendon commented. "I found Bo there too about the same time. I wonder if they knew each other?"

"They're friends. Don't you see?" Bailee said. "They *do* know each other."

"I believe they do. Well, I need to get going. Come on,

Bo. It was nice meeting you folks," Brendon said. "I promised my wife I'd buy a paper."

"It was nice meeting you, too," Mark said.

"Have a good day." Brendon nodded and turned to walk away, tugging on Bo. Something was nagging at him, like it was right before his eyes, so clear yet he couldn't put his finger on it. He put his head down, thinking. A random thought crossed his mind. What kind of dog did Lee have? It was a little white fluffy dog.

"Wait!" Brendon shouted.

Mark and Bailee turned around.

Brendon looked at the little dog. "Butterball? Is that you, Butterball?"

The little dog canted her head, hearing the familiar sounds. It had been a long time since anyone had said her name in a loving way. She came wiggling up to Brendon and licked his hand. Her round soulful eyes met Brendon's.

"You are Butterball!"

"Her name is Snowflake," Bailee said defiantly. She looked to her dad. "She's my dog."

"She is," Brendon confirmed.

"You know Snowflake?" Mark asked. His tone was one of concern.

"No. I knew her owner for a while, but he passed away." Brendon didn't plan on telling them the rest of the story. "I don't know how she ended up at the same rest stop, and I don't even want to guess. But I know she's in good hands now."

"I love her," Bailee said. "I'll always love her."

"I'm sure you will." Brendon pulled out his wallet. "Here's my card. If you ever need anything, give the station a call and ask for me. I'm happy to help."

"Thank you," Mark said. He looked at the card which read Department of Public Safety. "I'll be sure to keep this. By the way, I'm looking for a job. Are there any openings at the DPS?"

"There's one for a dispatcher. Stop by on Monday, and tell them I sent you."

"I'll do that. Thank you."

"Bye, Bo," Bailee said.

Brendon smiled and said, "Bye. Good luck to you folks and be sure to follow up on that job lead."

"You can be sure I'll do that."

It was Monday morning and the McMahon household was busy as everyone got ready for the day.

Allison checked her watch, making sure she had time to make it to her appointment. Josh finished breakfast, swung his backpack over his shoulder, and raced out the door to catch the school bus. Bo sat eagerly studying Allison's every move, waiting for a morsel to be tossed his way. Satisfied the kitchen was empty, Allison broke the last piece of bacon in half, gave one to Bo, then ate the other. "I'm eating for two," she explained to Bo, as if he understood her.

"Sorry I can't make the appointment this morning. We're short staffed," Brendon said.

"It's okay. I'll be alright without you."

He kissed Allison on the cheek, told her to have a good day, drive safe, keep the doors locked, watch where she walked, and some other things that he didn't quite remember at the moment.

Taking a handful of Bo's fur in his hand, he told Bo to stay with Allison and to not wander too far away. Bo returned affection by licking Brendon's hand.

Allison smiled, bid her husband a good day, and glowed with that look only expectant mothers have. Bo stood by, wagging his tail.

"Gotta run," Brendon said as he raced out of the house.

Today was the best day of Brendon's life, and dear

God did it ever feel good to be alive! There was a crispness in the air, like life had been reinvented, and he walked with his shoulders squared, an extra spring in his step.

Brendon approached every single day of his life like it would be the last one. Every minute, every second, nothing wasted on anxiety, hatefulness, or regret, for he considered each breath he took to be a gift.

He lavished his unwavering love on the ones closest to him, like he was a millionaire determined on spending his last dime.

Brendon had slept well the night before and the night before that, ever since he had faced his fiery demons that had been tearing away his soul. As an adult, he was able to face his silent tormentors who had finally been extinguished as sure as the flame on a match could not withstand a gallon of gushing water.

He was leading an innately satisfying life.

He was married, had a thirteen year old son, another on the way, and the thought of becoming a new father was foremost on his mind. Adoption papers for Josh were about to be finalized and he couldn't wait to sign them and make his blended family official.

He swore to be a good father and was anxious for the little tyke to be born and become old enough to play ball because the little tyke's old man had been a standout on the little league baseball team, playing shortstop, and breaking all sorts of local team records.

Once the light turned green, Brendon turned the cruiser onto the four-lane highway. He came to another stoplight and rolled the cruiser to a stop, listening to the radio crackling and the familiar voices of the dispatchers. It had been a slow day with not much to write home about, yet he never let his guard down because he had learned that the hard way. His hand went to his chest, placing it near his heart where scars remained a constant reminder of how close he had come to losing his life.

He thought about how in seeking forgiveness he had found the woman that would become his wife. She was the one who had saved him, who showed him how to live his life without regret, to move forward.

He ached for her when he was away, the touch of her hand, the smile on her face when the sun shone on her. He ached for their unborn son to make his debut in the world.

She had showed him to live in the moment, for the moment was what we really only have. Not yesterday's disappointments or tomorrow's dreams that may never come.

Right now.

This moment.

Here was all that anybody ever had.

She was the one who helped him face his demons in his nightmares, helped him squash those demons under the soles of his courage.

She was the one who gave him the courage to save her son in the raging fire.

She was the one who would love him forever, who would give him more children, who would grow old with him, who would cry and laugh with him, and share husband and wife moments that only two people who really know each other experience. They would forever share a deep love, an understanding love, an unselfish love.

She would be his one forever.

Allison McMahon lay on the examining table in the doctor's office, her head resting on the pillow, the ultrasound machine situated next to her. The nurse and doctor walked in, he in his white overcoat, his nurse dressed in blue scrubs and holding a medical tablet.

"How are you today, Mrs. McMahon?" the doctor asked.

"I'm fine. And you?"

"Great. Where's your husband?"

"He couldn't make it. Duty calls."

"I see. Are you ready to learn the baby's sex?"

"I am."

"Don't want it to be a surprise?"

"No, doctor, I don't like surprises. The due date is so close now and I need to get as many things ready as possible."

"Okay. This will be a little cold," he said referring to the ice cold jelly used to conduct the ultrasound images. He squirted a thin ribbon of jelly onto her belly, then using his left hand he pressed the ultrasound conductor onto her belly while looking at the monitor. "The baby's heartbeat is good. Everything is fine, the baby is perfect." He turned to look at Allison. "Are you sure you want to know?"

"Yes," she said, her anxiety rising.

"You're having a girl."

A girl.

Allison's eyes welled with tears and she blinked fast. "A girl? Are you sure?" She swallowed a lump in her throat.

"Positive," the doctor said. "Are you alright?"

Allison didn't hear the doctor, or notice the nurse wipe her belly with some paper towels. All she could think about was having a little girl and how much Madison would have liked to have been a big sister. The tears came easily, and the nurse handed her a Kleenex.

Maddy, you're going to have a little sister. Let me introduce you to Elizabeth Madison McMahon.

The End

Author's Note

Even though this story was fiction, the fire was real and happened during Labor Day weekend in September 2011. Myself, my husband, and youngest daughter were driving home along Highway 71, heading east from Austin to Houston where we live. Bastrop is located in a valley, and as we crested a hill, the smoke was unbelievable.

Cars were parked on the side of the road, people were taking pictures, and we debated whether or not to continue home. After a bit of discussion, we decided to head home on Highway 71 that cuts through the Lost Pines.

Towering pines line the road for several miles. It would be the last time we would see those pines. The fire incinerated the pines, and all that is left are burnt sticks in the ground. Several years later, the burnt sticks still remain, although life is indeed making a stand. Small saplings are growing, grass has returned, and the oak trees somehow managed to survive the fiery maelstrom.

The fire was blamed on strong winds caused by Tropical Storm Lee, creating ideal conditions for wildfires to spread. It was thought the high winds toppled trees which fell on overhead wires, causing sparks to ignite the dry gas and debris.

The fire, named the 'Bastrop Country Complex fire', scorched more than 34,000 acres, destroyed over 1,600 residential buildings, and killed two people. It was the most destructive wildfire in Texas history.

Grandma Jones' Cookie Recipe

Blake's grandmother's peanut butter "cooky" recipe—as mentioned in the novel, including the misspelled word!

1 cup salted butter, softened
1 teaspoon vanilla
1 cup brown sugar
1 cup white sugar
2 eggs
1 cup peanut butter
3 cups sifted flour
2 teaspoons baking powder
¼ teaspoon of salt

In a large bowl, cream butter and add sugar, creaming well. Add vanilla. Beat in eggs, mixing thoroughly. Add peanut butter and mix well. In a separate bowl, sift together flour, baking powder, and salt. Add flour mixture to the creamy mixture, a little at a time. Batter will be stiff.

Roll batter into small balls and place on a "cooky" sheet. Flatten and crisscross with tines of a fork.

Bake for 10 to 15 minutes in a pre-heated 375 deg oven.

Makes about 5 dozen cookies.

Read On!

Have you read Blake's other novels? If not, you're missing out!

Unspoken Bond was Blake's first novel, and won an honorable mention award in the Houston Writers Guild novel contest. It's a story about the love of two people transcending time and tragedy, and about the love of a dog that will never be forgotten. *Unspoken Bond* reached as high as number 21 in the Top 100 bestselling Kindle books. Really. She has the screen shot to prove it.

Miracle on Wolf Hollow Lane was Blake's second novel, and won second place in the Houston Writers guild novel contest. It's a story about one dog's power of fortitude and gritty determination to live, to beat the odds, to return home and maybe, just maybe, save her family she was born to protect. The novel also broke the Top 100 bestselling Kindle books.

Both *Unspoken Bond* and *Miracle on Wolf Hollow Lane* were inspired by real life events. In one, Blake rescued a starving puppy, the other one about a dog who was rescued after being been shot and left to die in the vast wilderness of South Texas.

Both books are available on Amazon as an eBook or paperback.

Unspoken Bond

Miracle on Wolf Hollow Lane

About the Author

Blake O'Connor is married and has two grown daughters. She lives in Houston with her husband, Alan, a small fourteen year old Chiweenie named Bat (or Babe, or whatever her name is at the moment), and two large cats named Boomer and Purry, who her daughter wrangled from the street. Cat wrangling is a profession. And she has a Corgi grandpup named Kiki.

When Blake isn't reading, writing, or dreaming up her next heart-warming story, you can find her gardening (or trying to), taking her dog walking on Buffalo Bayou, or enjoying the green space behind her house.

Blake loves to hear from her readers, so please feel free to email her or to send a Facebook friend request. Email is: blake.oconnor123@aol.com. Facebook is: Blake O'Connor-Author. She'll personally answer and will never share your email with anyone.

One Last Thing....

To my dear readers I am forever grateful that you took a chance on an Indie author and downloaded *Trust Me*. If you enjoyed *Trust Me* please let your friends know. A simple Facebook shout-out, or tweet, or mentioning this on your blog goes a long way.

And finally, the easiest way to help an author and to show your support is to write a review. Reviews are the way other readers determine whether or not they want to read the book. One or two sentences would be great. I'll be forever grateful if you could.

All the best,
Blake

68503594R00148

Made in the USA
Middletown, DE
30 March 2018